CLASSICAL MUSIC EXPLAINED

CLASSICAL MUSIC EXPLAINED

JOHN M. PUNT

John M. Punt Books

Contents

THE ROMANTIC ERA

IV
NATIONALISM

V
MODERNISM

VI
MUSICAL THEATRE

APPENDICES

To my educators,
parents, teachers, professors, and co-laborers
in the efforts to train minds and improve hearts, young and old.

To my children,
who fill me with a desire to teach and teach well
that we might see the gifts given to us also given to the future.

To my wife,
who encourages me to seek the Good, the True, and the Beautiful in all I do,
who loves me more than I deserve,
and who reminds me to do all Soli Deo Gloria.

I

The Baroque Era

THE AGE OF HUMANISM

1600-1750

I

Introduction

BAROQUE CHARACTERISTICS

Departing from the previous era of history, the Renaissance, the Baroque sought to dive further into the world created by humanism. A desire to go further than the Ancients with philosophy, art, architecture, and music becomes a driving force in the seventeenth century; and the cracks in the former monolith of the Church begin to show in the way that governments order themselves. Chief among these are the de-spiritualizing of literature and architecture and the display of mankind's prowess and attention to detail. These elements will carry over into music, but they can be seen easily in a comparison of architecture between the Renaissance and the Baroque.

MUSICAL CHARACTERISTICS

Musical characteristics of the period reflect the philosophical characteristics of the era. Like the Renaissance before it, the emphasis on humanist ideals brings secular music into the limelight and there is a great emphasis on **dance music** and its influence on all music, even music in the church. **Text painting** continues as a trend in vocal music. **Ornamentation** and sophistication become hallmarks of the style, but are reserved for musical or textual moments that require emphasis. Underneath all music, there is a consistent **rhythmic pulse** that moves the music forward and keeps both the listener and the performer grounded in the musical attitude conveyed. Like public speech of the day, there is an emphasis on form that is filtered through sound **rhetorical practices**.

Dance-Inspired Music
Text Painting
Ornamentation for Emphasis
Rhythmic Drive
Rhetorical Form

MAJOR COMPOSERS

Lully

Jean-Baptiste Lully (1632-1687) grew in his musical career in France under Louis XIV, The Sun King. Working his way up to the chief composer of France, he eventually had the sole right to publishing and approval of publishing for all of France, so his music set the standard for other composers in France. Chief among his works is the opera *Armide*.

Vivaldi

Antonio Vivaldi (1678-1741) rose to fame in his role at the *Ospedale della Pieta*, a school for female foundlings. There, he taught music and wrote hundreds of works for the Girls Orchestra there. Among his most famous works are the concertos entitled *The Four Seasons*.

Bach

Johann Sebastian Bach (1685-1750) was considered among the greatest composers even in his own age. His works include hundreds of keyboard works and church cantatas. He composed in every major genre except opera. Among his most famous works are the *Passions According to St. Matthew* and *St. John*.

Handel

George Frederic Handel (1685-1759) was the most cosmopolitan of this class of composers. He grew up in Germany, studied in Italy, performed in France, and was the court composer of England. His operas were highly dramatic, as were his oratorios and he wrote what is perhaps the most well known of all time: *Messiah*.

2

Jean-Baptiste Lully

THE BAROQUE DANCER

1632-1687

BIOGRAPHY

Lully was born in a small town in Italy and showed promise as a young man. He was likely born into poverty, though showed some intellectual prowess, as a travelling duke from France elected to pay his parents in order to receive Lully into his household. There, he received an education and built his skill as a musician.

In France, he was constantly employed in the orchestras of wealthy noblewomen. He was an excellent musicians and a talented composer, though he was usually dismissed from orchestras for using his compositional skill to write "scurrilous verses and tunes."

Eventually, Lully was placed into Louis XIV's service in the new ensemble, Le Quatre-Vingt Violons du Roi, and became the court composer to the Sun King. There, he wrote numerous ballets and operas and received the royal patent for music. Due to this, his music became the gold standard of music in France: his approval had to be placed upon any piece of music that was to be published (seldom anything besides his own). Not only did other composers imitate his style in order to earn publication, but his music was also highly influential in France and around the continent. He was among the first to popularize the idea that art music ought to revolve around dance patterns and styles.

Lully is an excellent starting point for understanding Baroque music: his music is minimally complex, but fully displays the characteristics of the Baroque and gives insight into the state of music before further developments of the era.

LE QUATRE-VINGT VIOLONS DU ROY

King Louis XIV, the Sun King of France, built Paris to become the new cultural capital of the world. His palace, Versailles, became the hub of art and music throughout Europe. His father began the 24 Violins of the King ensemble to further advance music. The ensemble was a sort of private orchestra to play for any special events, meals, daily rituals, etc. (The ensemble was not made of 24 violins, strictly speaking: the various names for violin, viola, alto viola, bass viola, and cello were all variations of the name violon in French.)

LULLY'S DEATH

Prior to the nineteenth century, few conductors used a baton — generally, orchestra leaders either played the harpsichord or beat a staff upon the ground in order to keep time. At one performance, he accidentally struck his own foot with the conducting staff and contracted gangrene. Doctors could have amputated his leg, but he refused to have his leg removed in order that he might continue to dance ballet. (His renown as a dancer was great: he once danced with the Sun King himself in a ballet, which may have sparked his appointment to the post of royal composer.) Lully died two weeks later from infection of the brain.

THE FRENCH OVERTURE

In the early Baroque era, most musical performances were restricted to the upper class. Few others had the economic means or the leisure time to avail themselves of art music. As such, the impetus for most people to attend an opera, ballet, or symphony was the invitation of the commissioning party (usually nobility or royalty). Therefore, the main point of attending for most was not to see the performance, but to be seen at the performance. People would spend their time reading, talking, sleeping: essentially doing anything that meant avoiding watching the performance.

In addition to the lack of attention on the drama presented on the stage, the attention was being turned toward those who entered the hall: many spectators began to arrive late to the performances, because they were thus able to be prominently seen by all in attendance (this is the origin of the term "fashionably late"). However, the king became increasingly frustrated that he was not the center of attention at his own operas and ballets.

The overture was increasingly problematic: it often served as a ten to fifteen minute cushion in which people could arrive fashionably late and ruin the king's grandiose appearance. What Lully wrote in response became known as the French Overture.

Lully restructured the overtures to all of the ballets and operas presented at Versailles. Instead of being a long, dreary work, Lully shortened the overtures to a two-to-three minute excerpt, sectioned them off into a ternary form, all of which was based on dance, and made the king the center of attention again. The slow-fast-slow form of the French Overture became universally accepted, and overtures of operas and ballets were now the grand revealer of who adored the king and who adored themselves. The overture to *Armide*, one of Lully's most famous operas, is a classic example of this three part structure. The middle dance section would feature the danced entrance of the Sun King, who often danced ballet on the way to his own box if he were not a soloist in the performance itself.

3

Antonio Vivaldi

THE BAROQUE SOLOIST

1678-1741

BIOGRAPHY

Antonio Vivaldi grew up in Venice, Italy, and studied music under his father, who was also a priest. Antonio also studied to enter the priesthood and served as a priest for a short stint until his asthma prevented The Red Priest (as he was called, due to his red hair) from fully engaging in his duties.

After leaving the priesthood, Vivaldi taught at the *Ospedale della Pieta*, a church-sponsored school for foundlings, or orphans. As music teacher, he conducted the orchestra and was able to use the orchestra as his compositional playground. He wrote hundreds of works for this orchestra, many of which were concertos (concerti): orchestral works featuring a skilled soloist. Some of the most famous of these are the four violin concerti that make up **The Four Seasons**. It is striking to consider that these works, which challenge the modern violinist, were written for a whole orchestra of teen-aged foundling girls.

Eventually, Vivaldi tried his hand at opera, with mixed success. One *impresario* (opera house-runner) worked to bring him to Austria, where his final opera failed. It was there that he died in poverty and obscurity.

THE FOUR SEASONS

Concerto

At the time Vivaldi was writing, the concerto was just taking off as a popular genre in music performance. The concerto, an orchestral work featuring a skilled soloist, provided an opportunity to showcase a composer's ability to skillfully employ the elements of form in a piece of music and to showcase the composer's ability to write technically demanding music for the soloists. Naturally, it also allowed the performer to showcase their abilities, which eventually showed the divide between the average performer and the virtuoso.

Poetry

The use of poetry in The Four Seasons is what makes the work centuries ahead of its time. In the late Romantic era, the schism between program music (music for the story's sake) and absolute music (music for the music's sake) appeared and widened, threatening the future of music as a cultural institution; but the mention of program music by name didn't occur until the mid-1800s. Vivaldi's music is clearly written with the stories of these four sonnets in mind.

It is unclear whether Vivaldi wrote the poetry himself, but the composer's employment of key ideas and figures shows a close attention to the details of the text. Vivaldi includes various species-specific birdsongs, hunting horn calls, and evocations of natural imagery (such as rain and thunderstorms) to heighten the dramatic intensity of the work. Because of his skill in adapting the poetry, there is no question that The Four Seasons stands as a masterwork of program music, nearly two hundred years early.

Below are the texts for one movement of each concerto. One could easily find a performance online and listen along and clearly hear the dramatic shifts from line to line in the poem. Vivaldi excellently portrays each with only the instruments in a string orchestra at the time.

Spring, Movement I

Festive spring has arrived,
The birds salute it with their happy song.
And the brooks, caressed by little Zephyrs,
Flow with a sweet murmur.
The sky is covered with a black mantle,
And thunder, and lightning, announce a storm.
When they are silent, the birds
Return to sing their lovely song.

Summer, Movement I

Under the heat of the burning summer sun,
Languish man and flock; the pine is parched.
The cuckoo finds its voice, and suddenly,
The turtledove and goldfinch sing.
A gentle breeze blows,
But suddenly, the north wind appears.
The shepherd weeps because, overhead,
Lies the fierce storm, and his destiny.

Autumn, Movement III

The hunters, at the break of dawn, go to the hunt.
With horns, guns, and dogs, they are off,
The beast flees, and they follow its trail.
Already fearful and exhausted by the great noise
Of guns and dogs, and wounded,
The exhausted beast tries to flee, but dies.

Winter, Movement I

Frozen and trembling in the icy snow,
In the severe blast of the horrible wind,
As we run, we constantly stamp our feet,
And our teeth chatter in the cold.

4

Johann Sebastian Bach

THE BAROQUE GENIUS

1685-1750

BIOGRAPHY

Bach grew up in a musical household, a product of generations of German musicians. Orphaned by age 10, young Johann studied under various family members, eventually beating out his own brother in a competition for an organist post.

Bach traveled little during his lifetime, never going beyond 200 miles of his birthplace. In that region, though, his compositions for churches, schools, and courts were widely known. His ability to write quickly led him to complete over 1000 works in his lifetime, most of which are multi-movement selections. His works were seldom performed more than once, though he often recycled musical ideas when another piece was needed on short notice.

Because Bach never ventured into the world of mainstream secular music (particularly opera) nor did he look to fame as his measure of success, his works did not find an international audience quickly. Bach thrived for nearly 30 years in Leipzig, but died in relative obscurity.

Bach married twice and had a total of twenty children, eight of whom died in childhood. Many of the sons went on to have successful music careers in the following decades.

Upon his death, sales of his printed music were so low that the publishers sold the copperplates used for engraving to C. P. E. Bach, one of Johann's sons, for a low price. He intended to sell them to help take care of the family, but some of these only-copies were melted down for the value of their metal.

Bach's name did not see a revival for nearly 75 years, when a young man by the name of Felix Mendelssohn discovered a library of Bach works in a church basement and sought to recover Bach's name and musical style for the next generation.

The Purpose of Music

Bach was a staunch Orthodox Lutheran and his music reflects his religious beliefs. At a young age, he set down his belief in the purpose of music:

**"THE AIM AND FINAL END OF ALL MUSIC SHOULD BE NONE OTHER THAN THE GLORY OF GOD
AND THE REFRESHMENT OF THE SOUL."**

This belief governed his creation of music and led him to create works that combined great drama with a high degree of complexity and invention. Bacch believed that since God is emotive, creative, and inventive, excellent music should reflect these qualities, thus giving God glory.

Each manuscript works concludes with the letters SDG -- "Soli Deo Gloria": "To the Glory of God Alone."

CANTATAS: BWV 140, "WACHET AUF"

Bach's hundreds of cantatas served as "sung sermons," as he called them. Bach worked with librettists to develop the dramatic theme from the Biblical text and distill the passage's teaching for the congregation, so they could understand its meaning upon the first listening.

In what is perhaps the most well-known of his cantatas, *Wachet auf, Ruft uns die Stimme*, Bach and the librettists explored marital themes from all across the Bible to make a cohesive narrative and commentary. It is characteristic of Bach for its use of various compositional techniques.

Wachet auf sings Christ's "Parable of the Ten Virgins." Ten bridesmaids are waiting in the middle of the night for the bridegroom to bring them to wedding feast; five of them did not come prepared with enough lamp oil to last the night. While they "made themselves ready" by going to buy oil, they missed the groom!

Crucial to note is Bach's dramatic use of soloists in the storytelling. The Alto soloist sings the role of the Soul; the Bass, Christ; the tenor, the Evangelist. The Chorus comments on the main theme of the passages, singing a refrain based on a popular Lutheran chorale. Bach reuses this chorale throughout the work to illustrate the continuity of the theme throughout the different texts. In this way, he explains the parables simply by recycling the music.

In the opening Chorale, the various voices call out to "Wake up!" at different times, with the sopranos singing a long version of the chorale tune. All voices merge on the word "Listen to the Voice!" Repetition and homophony emphasize the text "Wake up!" repeatedly. The melody of "it calls to us with a bright voice" rises and appears all over the chorus, just like the cries of the watchmen around the city walls. "Where, where, where, where are you, clever young Maidens?" has a rising, pleading tone, emphasized by its repetition.

Bach's brilliant dramatic use of the choir in a piece of church music heightens the congregation's understanding of the text, driving home the point of the sermon: "Make yourself ready" for the Great Wedding!

Audiences and congregations alike find Bach's brilliant exploration of the chorale tune stirring and memorable.

THE WELL-TEMPERED CLAVIER

Bach was not only a composer and avid performer of music, but an advocate for the furthering of musical developments. Renaissance tuning was still employed at the height of Bach's career, but a small movement was pushing for equal temperament -- the evening out of distance between pitches on the keyboard -- rather than for Pythagorean temperament (which provided acoustically perfect intervals, but only in a small number of keys).

In an effort to promote this development, Bach wrote a series of *24 Preludes and Fugues*, one for each of the 12 major and 12 minor keys that would be possible in the new tuning system. This work was widely published and studied, driving the adoption of even temperament, which lasts to the modern era.

5

George F. Handel

THE BAROQUE STORYTELLER

1685-1759

BIOGRAPHY

Handel grew up in a musical household in Germany, studying keyboard and composition from a young age. Even at this early age, he showed promise. He soon held a number of church jobs for organ and composition and premiered his first opera at the age of 20.

He next traveled to Italy, where he studied composition and was exposed to more and more opera, soon mastering the style. A ruler in Southern Germany was a frequent commissioner of Handel's music, which worked out serendipitously for Handel when this ruler became King George II of England. Handel moved to England and enjoyed great success and notoriety.

Handel is known for making oratorio successful, almost single-handedly. His use of the chorus-a- character and of the orchestra for furthering the dramatic thrust of the work greatly changed the operatic landscape, preparing the way for Mozart, Rossini, and Verdi.

A carriage accident in 1751 injured his eye. So did the surgery in 1752, which left him blind. It was performed by the same surgeon who attempted to heal Bach's glaucoma, instead leaving him with a fatal infection.

MUSICAL CHARACTERISTICS

Opera

At the height of Handel's career, opera had taken a great downturn in the public eye. Works like John Gay's *The Beggar's Opera*, which had little semblance of a plot but contained over 40 solo songs (many of which included eight to ten verses) left opera undesirable to the average audience member. Some documentation reveals that many audience members were more interested in their literature, their social appearance, or their lover seated next to them than to the drama on stage.

Handel's early operas were very cosmopolitan: French recitative in French, Italian arias in Italian, and German-style choruses in German -- but all in the same opera. While he did achieve a level of musical excellence, he distanced the audience from opera! This was characteristic of Handel operas until he united the musical effects in one dramatic story and in one language. These works stand as operatic hits to this day.

Oratorio

In the place of opera, Handel employed all of these techniques in oratorio (from the Latin, "to speak"). Oratorios were like church operas. They were sung in the vernacular, speaking forth familiar Biblical stories, with the dramatic and narrative force of opera. These drew great crowds, especially the most well-known of all oratorios: *Messiah*.

MESSIAH

The script for *Messiah*, also known as a libretto, was given to Handel by a friend. It is a reflection of the life of Jesus Christ, with tie-ins to all parts of the Bible. Handel began work on August 20 and completed the 2.5 hours of music in just 24 days.

Perhaps the most thrilling and convincing technique Handel employs in Messiah is text painting, when the music sounds like what the words say. Here is the technique used in the opening aria, "Ev'ry Valley."

The word "exalted" forms visual valleys, which are slowly lifted up from the beginning of the line to the end,

The "mountains and hills" are, in fact, made low,

"Crooked" is crooked, and "straight" is straight.

Similar treatments can be found all throughout the oratorio, with titles of pieces being interpreted quite literally, as well. "All We Like Sheep" is interpreted as a very difficult fugue, in which the choir sounds as though they have gone astray. "The Trumpet Shall Sound" prominently features a trumpet.

ZADOK THE PRIEST

Handel's famous coronation anthem is filled with the drama he achieved onstage, but on the grandest of scales -- the crowning of the English monarch at the nation's greatest church. The text is based on 1 Kings 1:38-40:

"Zadok the Priest and Nathan the Prophet anointed Solomon King. And all the people rejoiced, and said: 'God save the King! Love live the King! May the King Live Forever! Allelulia! Amen!'"

Handel introduces the work with a long, but gripping, orchestral prelude fit for the crown-regent's long walk down the aisle of Westminster Abbey and the music shifts from majestic march to celebratory dance to jubilant supplication, perfectly matching the text throughout.

Written for the coronation of King George II, the work has been performed at every British coronation since its composition in 1727.

II

The Classical Era

THE AGE OF ENLIGHTENMENT

1750-1820

6

Introduction

CLASSICAL CHARACTERISTICS

The Classical era in history deviates sharply from the Baroque in its desire to rely not merely on humanism, but on classicism. Where Baroque philosophers and architects sought to expand into new horizons of human understanding, Classical era practitioners looked back to Greek and Roman societies and use ancient input to shape modern ideals: use what has lasted throughout all of humanity to shape today. These elements will carry over into music, but they can be seen easily in a comparison of architecture between the Baroque and the Classical. Where sophistication and extremes led the way before, the Classical era turns to simplicity and elegance.

MUSICAL CHARACTERISTICS

Musical characteristics of the period reflect the philosophical characteristics of the era. Like the Renaissance, the emphasis on classical ideals brings philosophy into the center of music. **Symmetry** becomes a major fixture of Classical era music, reflecting the idea of **rhetorical balance**. You might conceive of this as "Question/Answer" form -- "Q/

A/Q/A" or "A/B/A/B" form. The orchestra grows significantly during the Classical era, and **instruments of the orchestra are highlighted individually** on a more regular basis. The music should reflect simplicity and accessibility by making **melodies short and memorable**. The memorability and accessibility of the music are only heightened by the watch words of **elegance and grace** in all music.

Interest in Symmetry
Rhetorical Form
Exploration of the Orchestra
Memorable Melodies
Elegance and Grace

MAJOR COMPOSERS

Haydn

Franz Joseph Haydn (1732-1809) became the premier composer of the Classical era as the "Father of the Modern Symphony" and composer of over 100 symphonies, and over 70 string quartets. His mastery of the new compositional language combined with his ability to teach made him highly influential throughout the era.

Mozart

Wolfgang Amadeus Mozart (1756-1791) is Classical music's greatest icon. A precocious young child, Mozart was proficient in any instrument he picked up, he wrote music from the age of six, and had a remarkable ability to stir up and elongate musical drama in innumerable ways.

Rossini

Gioachino Rossini (1792-1868) was the figurehead of early *bel canto* opera. His 39 operas, countless songs, chamber works, and brilliantly lively orchestrations brought Italy back to center stage at the start of the "primo ottocento." Ever the comic wit, Rossini's memorable melodies have lingered with audiences for centuries.

Beethoven

Ludwig van Beethoven (1770-1827) is known as the transitional figure between the Classical and Romantic eras. His inventiveness and exploration with motifs spurred on the kind of developments seen later in the period. With the death of Beethoven certainly came the death of the Classical era.

7

(Franz) Joseph Haydn

THE FATHER OF CLASSICAL MUSIC

1732-1809

BIOGRAPHY

Franz Joseph Haydn was born in Austria to a musical family and learned music from a young age. He was an avid keyboardist and violinist from his youth -- so much so that after a performance at the age of five, a nobleman approached his family to pay for his musical training. In those days, musical training accompanied a well-rounded education at a boarding school. Once he left for school at the age of six, he never returned home again due to the length of his education and subsequent success as a musician.

Many stories abound regarding Haydn's young life, many of them still regarded as true. In one such tale, the playful Joseph took a pair of scissors to the ponytail of the female chorister sitting in front of him. She did not notice until she was home. In another, 13-year-old Haydn's voice had changed and his services in the school's choir were no longer needed. The alternative was to voluntarily become a castrato. Haydn opted out of that solution, though his choirmaster had a different opinion -- one which Haydn escaped by jumping out the window!

After a number of years in local orchestras, singing studios, and small-time composing jobs, Haydn eventually came to the post of Orchestra Director to the royal orchestra of Prince Esterhazy of Austria. It was there that his career flourished and there that he remained for nearly 30 years, until the prince's death in 1791. His tenured position meant freedom to experiment without repercussion, and his unique style developed and stayed.

After this, he retired to London and finished writing the remainder of his 107 symphonies and 77 string quartets. His consistency of form and invention gave him the title "Father of the Modern Symphony."

THE PALACE OF ESTERHAZA

The Prince of Austria, Nikolaus Esterhazy, sought to display Austria's rich culture and abundant economy by mimicking another great prince of history -- King Louis XIV, "The Sun King." Nicolas recreated the palace of Versailles in modern-day Hungary.

Complete with 126 rooms, a ballet theatre, an opera house, a marionette theatre, and various other concert and recital halls, banquet halls, ballrooms, and much more; Esterhaza was an incredible architectural achievement and boasted the center of Austrian culture, at least that which was sponsored by the Prince. The palace's isolated location meant that little of the arts and culture created here left the grounds for public consumption. The isolation and massive debts accrued by the palace's construction also meant that after Nikolaus's death in 1790, no one occupied the castle until restorers took it up in the late 20th Century.

STRING QUARTET NO. 62, "THE EMPEROR QUARTET," MOVEMENT II

Haydn's music is known for its display of rhetorical, or "Question-Answer" Form. Nowhere is this more easily seen than in Haydn's

"Emperor Quartet," Movement II. This tune now forms the German national anthem, the main theme tune for the reunification of Germany in the 1840s.

By playing each two-measure phrase, one can begin to see the musical Questions and Answers that Haydn employs on the small scale to build up the larger theme. After "zooming out," one can see that the phrases form a larger Question-Answer structure. And by looking at the largest structure, one can see that the second half of the piece musically answers the first half. Haydn structures this work as a perfectly symmetrical, rhetorically-formed quartet.

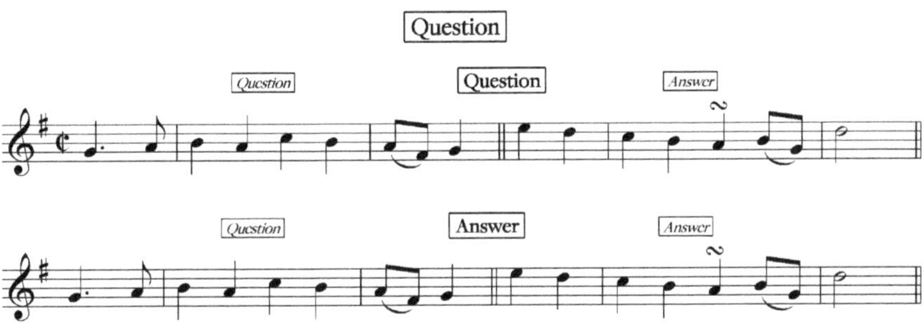

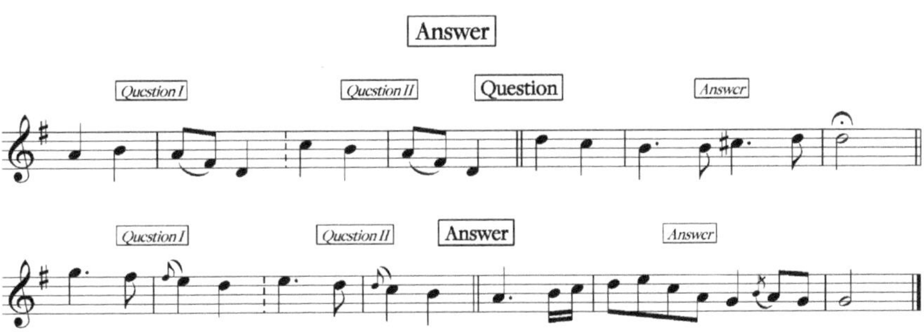

SENSE OF HUMOR

Haydn is also renowned for his excellent sense of humor, which shines through in pieces of music like the "Suprise" Symphony (No. 94, Mvt. II) and the "Joke" Quartet (Op. 33, No. 2).

The second movement of the "Surprise Symphony" opens with the theme, restates it at a pianissimo, and is interrupted by a number of whole-orchestra bangs, which successfully startle the audience almost every time!

The Joke Quartet concludes with a number of "Grand Pauses" between musical lines. When the audience thinks the piece is over, it turns out it isn't; when the audience thinks it will keep going, it's actually done! The joke is also on the performers, who do not have each other's parts on their own scores and are surprised when no one is playing!

8

Wolfgang Amadeus Mozart

THE PRODIGY OF CLASSICAL MUSIC

1759-1791

BIOGRAPHY

Wolfgang Amadeus Mozart was born into a musical family on Salzburg, Austria and thrived in the environment. His father was Europe's premier violin pedagogue, having written a widely popular and successful violin methodbook, and was an excellent composer in his own right. His sister, Maria Anna (or "Nannerl," as he called her), was also an excellent composer and violinist. Wolfgang was playing piano by the age of three, playing back music from memory at the age of five, and composing symphonies at the age of six and a complete opera at the age of 13.

He excelled, but knew he needed guidance, and in his teenage years, he travelled to Vienna to study composition with Haydn. After this move, his reputation as a composer and a pianist exploded. He constantly wrote symphonies, operas, and chamber works.

Mozart's most famous works are his operas, symphonies, and

concertos. The piano concerti, in particular, were clearly written for Mozart's own performance and a number of historical documents attest to his masterful performances.

Mozart died at the age of 35, while working on a Requiem co-missioned by an unknown person. Much of the portrayal from popular media has been debunked by recent scholarship, including the idea that Mozart was poisoned by another Viennese composer, Antonio Salieri. It was likely they were actually close friends and colleagues and that Mozart more likely died of a chronic kidney disease.

MUSICAL CHARACTERISTICS

Mozart's music has three main characteristics that carry through almost all of his work: symmetry, surprise, and simplicity.

Symmetry

Mozart's music is very much a product of its time. The principles of balance and symmetry according to rhetorical principles are seemingly binding upon the composer. The structure tends to be predictable, but what Mozart does within that structure can vary.

Surprise

While the consistency of form is very high, Mozart often finds a way to subvert expectations before the climax of a musical phrase. He often uses dominant seventh chords and augmented sixth chords as a means to extend the cadence and elongate the drama.

Simplicity

Mozart's music is undoubtedly idiomatic for each instrument or voice. He knew the practical effects of various techniques and employed these with careful attention, and always as a means to fulfill the drama.

SYMPHONY NO. 40 IN G MINOR

The summer of 1788 was a miserable one for Mozart. His most recent opera, Don Giovanni, was not met with critical success, money troubles were upon him, and his six-month-old daughter just died. In the midst of these circumstances, Mozart wrote three symphonies in the following three months, perhaps as a means to process his grief. The second of these, Symphony No. 40 in G Minor, is one of Mozart's greatest masterpieces.

The key of G Minor is itself a unique choice. This is one of only two minor key symphonies of Mozart's 41. The key was associated with grief and lamentation and it seems an appropriate selection here. The work seems to begin in media res, with a rustling in the violas, followed by a sighing lament in the violins — the theme for the loose sonata form to follow.

Mozart uses this lament theme as the main theme for the symphony, but it is coupled with another, more hopeful theme. It is the unique balance between these two and the way in which he incorporates them into a sort of dual-sonata form that gives the listener a peek into the unique qualities of Mozart's music.

Sonata Form

This symphony is structured around a loose, but generally true-to-form, sonata structure. The piece opens with this weeping motif, accompanied by a slightly longer meandering tune in the strings and a conclusive tutti orchestra strike. Strangely, Mozart shifts to the relative major key, B-flat Major, at the end of the exposition, rather than going to the dominant, D Major. This foreshadows the extreme harmonic development Mozart employs in the Development section of the sonata form, far different from his harmony in other works, as seen below.

Rather than explore the long theme in a small number of related keys, Mozart employs this weeping motif in nearly a dozen different keys before he returns "home" for a false recapitulation. The piece never commits to a note-for-note recap, but settles in a very abrupt modulation and brief restatement of the original key.

Typical Sonata Form

Symphony No. 40, Movement I

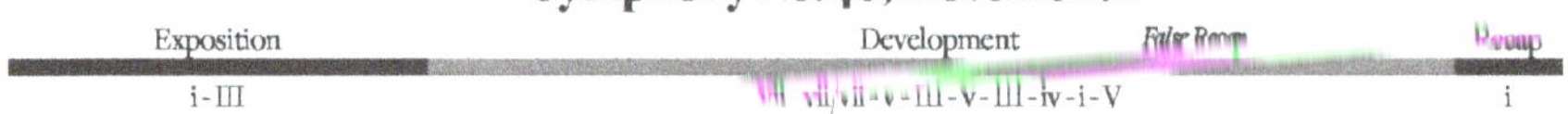

With these constant harmonic shifts, halting form decisions, and false and abrupt recapitulations, Mozart leaves the audience feeling unsettled by the end of the first movement. This not only foreshadows Beethoven's sonatas, but program music of the Romantic era with all of its intensely dramatic flair.

9

Gioachino Rossini

THE COMIC OF CLASSICAL MUSIC

1792-1868

BIOGRAPHY

Rossini grew up in an Italian household very encouraging of his musical talents. He began composing at the age of twelve and by the age of eighteen had written his most famous opera. Over the course of the next 13 years, he would write a total of thirty-four operas, generally at a rate of two to four operas per year.

Rossini wrote in both of the most famous operatic stylistic conventions: *opera buffa* — comic opera — and *opera seria* — serious opera. The traditional layman's distinction is that an *opera buffa* ends with a wedding whereas *opera seria* culminates in death. While Rossini's more serious works have not become the most well-known of his works, they have certainly endured the test of time.

His final opera, *Guillaume Tell*, or *William Tell*, was written in 1829, when he was just 37 years old. After the rampant success of this opera, Rossini retired to Paris and did not compose again for nearly twenty years. It is likely that the combination of wealth, poor health, and the rising public appeal of French grand opera led to his decision to "quit while he was ahead." Even for Europe's most-performed opera composer, it was difficult to compete with large orchestrations and live elephants on the stage!

Eventually, Rossini began to write again, only on the small scale. His later chamber music was collected in a set he published with the title *The Sins of My Old Age*. Among the most well known of these are the vocal quartets, chief of which is the famous "La Passeggiata." The collection is a marvelous exploration of music that shows that his early retirement was not due to a lack of skill.

ROSSINI'S MUSIC

Rossini's music can be divided roughly into two eras of composition.

Early Music

Rossini's earlier music tends to be in the arena of comic opera. His work here is largely done in the vein of Beethoven: he employs standard Classical forms with memorable melodies and alters the form for dramatic, often comic, effect. This is the standard practice in The Barber of Seville, which seldom features innovative harmonies, but generally resorts to the standard Italian cavatina-cabaletta aria structure. This form allows his characters to shine with dramatic exposition, while giving the singers themselves the spotlight to showcase the vocal prowess Rossini's music generally requires.

Later Music

At the beginning of the second act of La Cenerentola (Cinderella), the audience is taken to an entirely new realm of music. Not only is the story in a different place, but Rossini has ushered in the Romantic era with a few simple-but-stunning bars of music. His later works are far more harmonically exploratory, texturally innovative, and melodically enchanting. No longer reliant on comedy and vocal prowess, but on the composer's role as story-teller, Rossini's later music lays the groundwork for his successor, Verdi.

IL BARBIERE DI SIVIGLIA (THE BARBER OF SEVILLE)

An excellent introductory opera, *The Barber of Seville* has withstood the test of time as one of the most frequently performed operas in all of history. It is based on the first of the three Figaro plays by French playwright Pierre Beaumarchais, the second of which inspired Mozart's *The Marriage of Figaro.*

Synopsis

In Seville, Spain, a wealthy nobleman by the name of Count Almaviva is in love with the beautiful Rosina and has hired a small band to accompany him as he sings outside her window. She is locked away in the home of her legal guardian, Doctor Bartolo, who plans to marry her. Desparate for a solution, Count Almaviva finds the local barber, Figaro (at the time, barbers were general Fix-It Men), and recruits his help in devising a plan to free and marry her.

The first attempt finds Almaviva dressing up as a drunk soldier named Lindoro. A soldier, so that he can demand he stay in the house through the use of billeting orders; drunk, so that any advances toward Rosina or discourtesies toward Doctor Bartolo can be dismissed as the stupor of a man under the influence of alcohol. He takes on the name Lindoro so Rosina will love him for who he is and not for his status. Eventually, "Lindoro" creates such a disruption that the police are called in and the cover is blown. At that point, all those privy to the deception try to convince Bartolo that he is having some kind of hallucination and needs to rest. They succeed, but he is still wary of the fabled Count Almaviva on the loose somewhere in the city.

Doctor Bartolo enlists the help of the local priest and music teacher,

Don Basilio, to spread a rumor about Almaviva and drive him out of town. In the meantime, Almaviva dresses up as a subsitute music teacher "in the sick Don Basilio's absence" and shows up to give Rosina her lesson. Their cover is almost blown again when Don Basilio shows up, but is bribed to return home and fein illness. They are finally caught when, despite Figaro's efforts to distract the Doctor with a shave, they sing too loudly of our love and Almaviva is chased out of the house.

Doctor Bartolo discovers the letter from Almaviva and convinces Rosina that Lindoro is feining love for her in order to kidnap her and marry her to the Count (since she only knows about "Lindoro," not Almaviva). The Count and Figaro sneak in through the window at midnight to elope, but someone kicks out the ladder, preventing their escape. Meanwhile, the marriage documents have been prepared for Bartolo and Rosina, but the Doctor is nowhere to be found, so Almaviva and Rosina sign them, becoming husband and wife. Bartolo enters from his watch outside, pleased at having just taken down the ladder and trapping the intruder, but dismayed to discover that removing their escape route was "A Useless Precaution." In the end, all celebrate the wedding and the Count and Countess move to the countryside where they can be found in other operas written on the remaining Beaumarchais plays.

Music

As previously mentioned, most of the opera's music comprises arias in a two-part structure. The first part is a simpler song form with a lyrical melody and a little embellishment. The second part is faster and flashier, full of melismas and vocal effects.

A worthwhile exercise to demonstrate the difficulty of these arias would be to show a video which matches a performance with a scrolling score. Suggested arias include "Ecco ridente in cielo," "Largo al factotum," "Una voce poco fa," "La Calunnia," "A un dottor della mia sorte," and "Ah, il piu lieto."

10

Ludwig van Beethoven

THE INNOVATOR OF CLASSICAL MUSIC

1770-1827

BIOGRAPHY

Ludwig van Beethoven's childhood was not an easy one. Born in Bonn, Germany to a house of musicians, he struggled to fit into the family's musical heritage. While his grandfather was known as Bonn's most famous musician — a great composer in his own right — his father was a singer in the employ of the local magistrate, but was better known as the town drunk.

Ludwig's father's abuse shaped him in many ways, but the effect it had on his music was highly influential. His father held him to a high standard in practicing music, so much so that he locked the young boy in his room to practice piano for many hours a day. If the father heard any improvisation coming from upstairs, he would punish the young pianist for "not sticking to the page." His philosophy was that a great musician is someone who plays exactly what the composer desires.

For much of music history, this was true, but practices were changing in the wake of Mozart's piano concertos. Where previous pianists would have performed the composer's cadenzas, Mozart's improvised cadenzas opened up a new avenue for displaying virtuosity — one which no one could match until Beethoven came along.

In 1787, Beethoven moved to Vienna to study with the greatest composer of the age: Mozart; but he swiftly returned home when he heard of his mother's fatal illness. In 1792, he returned to Vienna, at which point Mozart had already died. He then studied under Haydn and Salieri.

BEETHOVEN'S LATER MUSIC

In 1802, he first wrote about his hearing loss in the *Heiligenstadt Testament*, written while recovering in a German resort town. Here, he writes with great hubris about the purpose of an artist and the challenge of his oncoming deafness. Whether Beethoven ever went completely deaf, we do not know, though recent scholarship suggests it was unlikely. Certainly, hearing loss was detrimental to his work, but clearly not detrimental to his musical output: his later works are decades ahead of their time.

Beethoven's musical experimentation is driven by motivic exploration. A motif — a recurring musical element that builds a theme — is repeatedly recycled in any possible permutation before moving on to a new exploration. His music is driven by narrative and he uses the Classical forms and harmonies only as a framework on which to build musical interest and drama.

This kind of motivic development can be seen as early as his first published work, String Quartet No. 1, but it is also clearly evident in the various sonatas — "Moonlight," "*Pathetique*," and "*Appassionata*" — and in the famous Symphony No. 5 in C Minor, subtitled “Fate.” In the exposition of the first movement alone (approximately two minutes) the famous “Fate knocking” motif can be heard over sixty times!

SYMPHONY NO. 5 IN C MINOR, "FATE"

There is perhaps no better piece than Beethoven's Symphony No. 5 to illustrate the bridge between the Classical and the Romantic. There is also perhaps no more familiar work to untrained audiences. Beethoven's use of a single motif and its development foreshadows the coming Romantic era.

The opening statement of the Symphony is one of the most famous lines in all of music, and it has been suggested that this is the sound of the titular Fate knocking on Beethoven's door (perhaps in correlation to the deepening of his hearing loss in the previous years):

Beethoven's dramatic flair is on full display here as the knocking of Fate becomes incessant. In merely twenty measures, he employs this rhythmic ostinato thirteen times — unprecedented by previous composers. Beethoven's memorable melodies and impactful music are due in large part to his ability to craft short, memorable motifs and employ them carefully and repeatedly in a way that actively shapes the form of the piece. Beethoven's use of this motif is a dramatic element gives the listener the impression that Fate cannot be held off by the symphony's protagonist. Looking forward to the end of the first movement, we see that it concludes with the same motif (on the nearly three-hundredth occurence).

Foreshadowing

In examining the opening bars, Beethoven's exploration of the orchestra with every instrument in his arsenal is a furthering of the Classical era's exploration of the orchestra. Where Mozart used various instruments in pairings and as soloists in concertos, Beethoven and later Romantic era composers (like Berlioz and Wagner) use individual instruments to communicate their musical themes in countless variations.

Beethoven's harmonies closely follow the harmonic model set by Mozart in Symphony No. 40. Not only does Beethoven's first movement mirror the altered sonata form of Mozart's first movement, the harmonic influences are clearly evident in the chromatic and borrowed chords from neighboring keys.

There is no question that Beethoven serves as the bridge between the Classical and Romantic eras and beyond.

III

The Romantic Era

THE AGE OF PASSIONS

1820-1900

II

Introduction

ROMANTIC CHARACTERISTICS

As Europe moved through the nineteenth century, the lasting impact of the Classical Era could be felt in many ways. The American and French Revolutions of the past paved the way for the unifications in Italy and in Germany; the sought-for *egalité* destabilized monarchies and aristocracies across Europe, heightening the role of the common man. This democratization of power meant that what was popular among the people became popular in art. Thus, common people and their common problems, myths, fairy tales, and the power of nature in the face of advancing science all became the subject of popular media. This is the age of The Brothers Grimm, *Les Misérables*, *The Count of Monte Cristo*, *Crime and Punishment*, and *Frankenstein*; these themes are easily seen in visual art, as well.

MUSICAL CHARACTERISTICS

The music of the Romantic era reflects the patterns set by literature, art, and poetry. The era of self-expression paved the way for **emotionally expressive music**, in contrast to the emotional restraint of the Classical era. The influences of art and philosophy led to the use of **extremes**, particularly of range and dynamics, but also of form and timbre. The influence of the Classical era remained as **melodies were memorable**, often derived from folk songs and folk stories. The popularity of folk stories such as those collected by the Brothers Grimm, or the supernatural stories promoted by the likes of Goethe (in *Faust*), led to a popular interest in **dramatic music**. As the century developed, so did the concept of the ***virtuoso*** and the expectation that all musicians become *virtuosi*.

Emotionally Expressive
Uses Extremes
Memorable Melodies
Story-Driven
Virtuosic

MAJOR COMPOSERS AND THEIR WORKS

Schubert

Franz Schubert (1797-1828) was an Austrian school teacher, pianist, and composer. His proclivity toward Beethoven's dramatic music and toward great poetry led him to be known as the creator of German art song, or lied. The birth date of art song is known as the day he composed his first song, *Gretchen am Spinnrade*.

Chopin

Frederic Chopin (1810-1849) was Poland's premier composer in an era when Polish culture was fading after Napolean's invasion. His stylistic interpretations of traditional Polish dances maintained Polish culture and preserved nationalistic fervor. Perhaps most well known are the *Minute Waltz* and the *Revolutionary Etude*.

Paganini

Niccolo Paganini (1782-1840) was known as The Devil's Composer due to the manner in which he extended the possible techniques and capabilities of the violin. With his physical ailments and extraordinary ability, he almost single-handedly create the idea of a virtuoso. His *24 Caprices* remain challenging today.

Brahms

Johannes Brahms (1833-1896) is a mainstay of classical music and a leader in nationalistic representation in music. His adherence to Classical structures while developing Romantic expression made him a unique force in the Traditionalist camp against the Progressives of the era. His *Symphony No. 1* is largely reflective of this.

Liszt

Franz Liszt (1811-1886) is widely regarded as the first rock star of classical music. His refined skill, raw power, and showmanship at the piano paved the way for more widespread popular adoption of Progressivist music, as well as a revival of the lesser-known composers he championed. Typical of his style is *Hungarian Rhapsody No. 2*.

Berlioz

Hector Berlioz (1803-1869) was a wildly innovative composer largely responsible for the resurgence of French music in the Romantic era. His self-taught composition and orchestration skills became the model for a new generation of dramatically expressive composers. All of this work can be seen in his masterpiece *Symphonie Fantastique*.

Verdi

Giuseppe Verdi (1813-1901) was the leader of Italian *risorgimento* music. As Italian unification moved forward, Verdi's music offered an outlet for the political yearnings of the generation, catapulting him to fame. His dramatic brilliance is consistently on display in every one of his later operas, particularly his Shakespearean operas — the music always serves the drama. *Rigoletto* remains an audience favorite for its memorable melodies and intense drama.

Wagner

Richard Wagner (1813-1883) is perhaps the most influential composer of all time. Taking the Progressivist musical tendencies to new extremes, Wagner pushed music, both harmonically and dramatically, to new heights. His understanding of the role of composer as author of the work paved the way for composers and film makers of the twentieth century. He considered *Parsifal* his greatest work, a truly stunning culmination of stage and sound.

Puccini

Giacomo Puccini (1858-1924) was broadly considered to be Verdi's successor in Italian opera. The leader of the *verismo* (realism) movement in opera, he brought opera's stories to the masses, both in subject and emotion. His orchestrations and his short, memorable arias (which fit onto the brand new vinyl records) made his exceptional music more accessible to a larger audience than any composer before. None of his works is better known than *La Bohème*, which remains one of the most frequently performed operas of all time.

12

Franz Schubert

THE ROMANTIC SINGER

1797-1828

BIOGRAPHY

Franz Peter Schubert grew up in a Viennese home centered on education. His father was a schoolmaster and upon graduation, Franz became a teacher at the school for a short period. He had a penchant for good poetry and always loved diving into high quality literature. Coupling this with his music education, Schubert followed the example of his musical idol, Beethoven.

Where Beethoven had written the first ever *liederkreis*, or song cycle, in *An Die Ferne Geliebte*, Schubert desired to take the concept further, turning music not only into short bursts of drama, heightening the meaning of a word here and there; but into extended dramatic journeys, wherein the narrative is always supported by the music — a sort of lived-in feeling in the music.

Schubert's music requires a skilled actor-singer and he found one in his singing partner Johann Michael Vogl. Vogl was a storied operatic baritone who excelled in the dramatic singing of music like Schubert's. Together, they performed many a *Schubertiade*, or Schubert-Song Evening, in which the two musicians would premiere many of the composer's new works, including a famous debut of *Erlkönig*.

Schubert and Beethoven lived in the same city for decades and though Schubert frequently passed his hero on the street, he was too shy to speak or seek advice. On Beethoven's death in 1824, Schubert's fellow composers named him the true successor to Beethoven, a token he must have appreciated — his fulfilled dying wish was to be buried next to the man who inspired his greatest achievements in music.

SCHUBERT'S MUSICAL INFLUENCE

Prior to Schubert, most composers writing art songs, or lieder, wrote primarily for the singer and used the piano as a sort of background instrument, outlining the harmonic structure and occasionally adding extra features for a unique effect.

Schubert's innovation and importance, though, is in his expressive use of the piano as a dramatic element in the musical storytelling of singing. As some have said, Schubert elevated the piano to equal with the singer, or to put it another way, he made the piano a character in the music alongside the singer.

Schubert almost always used the piano in this unique way. His song cycles, *Die Schöne Müllerin* and *Winterreise*, use motif-like elements throughout the cycles to convey the parts of The Brook and of the Wanderer's Footsteps, respectively. By using the piano as a dramatic character in the music, Schubert allows the audience to be immersed in the story of the music, even if that story lasts for sixty or ninety minutes over twenty-four songs.

In this way, Schubert was a major influence on the coming Romantic era, in which almost every piece of music is made to serve the story, rather than the story being subservient to the pleasantness of music.

ERLKÖNIG (THE SHADOW-KING)

Perhaps Schubert's most well-known and most-often performed single song, *Erlkönig* is based on a poem by German poet Johann Wolfgang von Goethe (the entire poem and its translation can be found in Appendix C). The poem tells the story of a father seeking help for his young boy on the verge of death, beckoned to the grave by the Shadow-King. An interesting exercise to compare this to Carl Loewe's version, composed a matter of months prior to Schubert's. Loewe's version is very traditional, where Schubert's is highly dramatic.

Schubert employs the vocalist in a new and dramatically innovative way. Here, there are four characters all sung by just one singer — quite a feat to accomplish; traditionally, this would have been broken up for four singers or would have been ignored, as it was in Loewe's composition. Schubert, however, gives a different vocal range to each of the characters, so they can be identified by their singing register as the piece goes on. He also assigns to each its own modality, either major or minor, coupled with a tonal center.

- The Narrator is generally fixed in G Minor and in a middle register of the voice, so as to remain fairly neutral.
- The Father sings largely in a reassuring major key, low in the voice, often striving to convince himself that he can dismiss his Son's visions.
- The Son sings with a desparate heartbeat in the piano, constantly rising in tonal center, much like his rising anxiety.
- The Shadow-King sings a lilting melody in major mode, very enticing to the Son.

Schubert, as expected, utilizes the piano as a character in the music, as well. The horse itself can be heard galloping whenever one of the three physical characters is singing. The horse disappears when the spirit Shadow-King is present, as if the listener has also been transported to this other dimension.

Schubert heightens the drama by reserving the destiny of the child for the final, slowed measure.

GRETCHEN AM SPINNRADE (*GRETCHEN AT THE SPINNING WHEEL*)

Composed on October 19, 1814, also known as the Birthdate of Art Song, *Gretchen am Spinnrade* was the first of Schubert's art songs and the start of an entirely new genre of music.

Here, as in *Erlkönig*, Schubert employs the piano to dramatic effect. In this case, the piano plays an almost constant rhythmic and melodic device to simulate the spinning of a spinning wheel.

The brilliance of this work is not only the elevation of the piano to equal character, but the insight into the mental state of the character singing the song. The song is sung by a girl who has lost her love and cannot focus on her work as she thinks of him (the entire poem and its translation can be found in Appendix C).

When she sings of "his words's // Magic flow, // His handholding // And, ah, his kiss!" the spinning wheel stops, remains silent, and slowly returns to spinning, just as a spinning wheel would take time to gain momentum again once it stopped. Schubert's innovation here is complete immersion in the story.

13

Niccolo Paganini

THE ROMANTIC VIRTUOSO

1782-1840

BIOGRAPHY

The young Paganini grew up in Italy and studied violin with his father. Beginning at the age of eleven and throughout his teenage years, he toured Europe, giving solo performances. During this time, he studied with the greatest teachers in Italy, each of whom sent him to their own teacher. He was utterly dedicated to the violin, sometimes practicing as much as 15 hours per day. His last teacher suggested that, with his mastery over the violin, he consider composing as another means of musical creativity.

At the age of 15, he became legally emancipated and led a lifestyle of womanizing and debauchery, bringing himself to poverty with gambling debts. At one point, he pawned his violin to pay his debts and was gifted another for his talent. He soon suffered a mental breakdown, probably due to his alcoholism. After overcoming this, he toured Europe for most of his life and became increasingly wealthy and influential. He retired to France to teach and compose, but his health caught up with him — he died of tuberculosis, syphilis, and larynx cancer at the age of 57.

Paganini's innovations in violin technique not only opened up new avenues for performance and composition, but drove the roles of both composer and performer in the popular eye. His techniques paved the way for the concept of the virtuoso and raised the bar for all performers in the following century.

PAGANINI'S REPUTATION

Paganini led the way in innovative techniques for the violin, but his fame and reputation did make enemies. Rumors abounded in Paganini's wake of his relationship with the devil or his Faustian deal. Among these were:

Paganini's mother sold his soul to the devil to ensure he would be a great violinist.

The violin was an instrument already associated with the devil and Paganini had great skill.

Paganini had murdered a woman and used her intestines as violin strings. Her soul was imprisoned within the instrument and it still screamed in the middle of performances.

Paganini developed false harmonics, which allowed him to play notes higher than anyone could before.

His deal with the devil gave him a demonic appearance and kept him from receiving last rites.

Paganini probably had both Marfan Syndrome (which elongates ones limbs and features) and Ehlers-Danlos Syndrome (which deteriorates connective tissues and makes one very flexible). He refused last rites because he did not think he was nearing death.

The devil assisted him in playing at concerts.

Paganini developed *left hand pizzicato* and ricochet, which allowed him to play notes with the "bow hand" hand — the hand no one was watching. It likely looked like as though the notes came out of nowhere.

24 CAPRICES FOR SOLO VIOLIN, OP. 1, NO. 24

Paganini's *Caprices* are renowned for their difficulty, but also for the new techniques Paganini explored in their composition. Paganini composed these works, written for his own performance, in small groups of pieces from 1802 to 1817, in the early part of his career.

The works are *études*, or studies, in various extended techniques. Each caprice-étude focuses on a single technique, many of which were pioneered by Paganini. Accordingly, they are studies in arpeggios, detache, octaves, triple- and quadruple-stops, ricochet, drone-and-melody, fast passagework, parallel thirds and tenths, spiccato, and more. Caprice No. 24 is likely the most popular, as its melody is straightforward and memorable, and it is repeated often in this Theme and Variations work. This, also, functions as an étude for many further Paganini-derived techniques, listed below:

I. Slurred legato passagework
II. Rapid shifting between strings, including open strings
III. Parallel octaves on adjacent strings
IV. Fast passagework on a single string
V. Spiccato passagework
VI. Parallel thirds and tenths on adjacent (even open) strings
VII. String crossings in fast passagework
VIII. Triple stops on distant strings
IX. Left hand pizzicato and *détaché*
X. All notes played on a single, high string
XI. Double stops and string crossings
XII. Slurred arpeggiations, double stops, and parallel sixths

Perhaps the most fascinating of these techniques is the Left-Hand *pizzicato*, the probable origin of the rumor that the devil assisted his playing. Most pizzicato was plucked by the right hand, so when audiences saw his right hand continuing to bow *arco*, but heard *pizzicato* notes arise from the instrument, they no doubt wondered whence the sound came. The use, not only in one instance, but in quick succession of the technique in Variation 9 is astounding.

14

Frédéric Chopin

THE ROMANTIC POET

1810-1849

BIOGRAPHY

Frédéric (or Fryderyk) Chopin was born to a French father and Polish mother in Warsaw. His musical parents encouraged his study on the piano, an instrument to which he was always and almost exclusively drawn. His first works were published in his teenage years, when he was already a renowned local artist, sponsored by a local prince (whose brother would sponsor him later in life).

At the age of 19, he was touring Europe and giving concerts to wide audiences who fell in love with the dashing and gregarious romantic. His friendships with Schumann and Liszt helped shape his music, which is often characterized as consistently flawless. His successes and positive critical reviews allowed him financial success and he grew to love the finer things in life.

Despite his move to Paris, the epicenter of the culture of arts, his heart remained in Poland, which was then under siege by Russia. His works have a pronounced nationalistic character, often based on folk music and dances of Polish culture. His work and his performances were often dedicated to the people of Poland. Chopin's music remains a defining example of stylized nationalistic music, regardless of era, and earned him the name "Poet of the Piano."

GEORGE SAND AND CHOPIN'S DEATH

The only lasting romantic relationship Chopin ever had was that with George Sand. George was the pseudonym of Amandine Aurore Lucie Dupin, the Baroness Dudevant, a famous novelist, celebrated by literary critics. Much of her public life was taken up with social activity; she herself wished that she were a man and typically wore the traditionally male attire of suit and waistcoat.

Chopin met Sand in Paris just before he foreswore love and the two spent the next decade together, though they never married. Chopin's poor health made him more pitiable to George, who considered him her pet project to nurse back to health. One of her gifts to him in this vein was a vacation to Majorca, Spain, to heal in the Mediterranean climate.

Unfortunately, their visit occurred during a rare wet season, which only inflamed Chopin's tuberculosis and other respiratory issues. They eventually returned to France, where Chopin resided at Sand's home in the countryside. Eventually, Sand recognized the lost cause of healing Chopin and departed from him. Within two years, he had lost his will to live and succumbed to his illness.

THE "REVOLUTIONARY" ÉTUDE

Chopin's *études* are not the same sort as those that came before him. Along with Liszt, Chopin transformed the *étude* from a scholarly piece, a "study," to a performance-ready concert piece. The origins of the genre lie in the need to create pieces that, with diligent practice, would strengthen skills necessary for the competent (or later, virtuoso) performer. Chopin's works still place an emphasis on technical skill, particularly the excellent use of legato playing; but Chopin wrote *études* that are lyrical and strikingly beautiful.

Perhaps the most well known of the Chopin *études* is Op. 10, No. 12, subtitled "Revolutionary." Chopin seems to have written this piece about the time of the November Uprising in 1831, a Polish revolution against the occupying Russian forces. When Warsaw fell to the Russians upon the revolution's failure, Chopin is reported to have said, "All this has caused me much pain. Who could have foreseen it?" Chopin's love of country shines through in this furious and passionate work.

The brief piano solo in C minor opens with a dominant chord and flurry of tumultuous activity in the left hand (the technique in focus for this work). After Chopin sets the canvas with the rumbling sixteenth notes in the bass, he then calls forth the famous melody, evoking a great and heroic struggle. The opening is recapitulated in the final line, which terminates in a C major chord, picturing the triumph of Polish nationalism, even in the face of military defeat. Chopin would make few public appearances later in life, but the proceeds of his later concerts went to Polish refugees and charities.

FOLK DANCES IN CHOPIN'S MUSIC

Particularly puzzling to the Western listener are some of the titles of Chopin's various genres -- polonaise, mazurka, and nocturne. These are all derived from Polish traditions.

Polonaise: originating as a uniquely Polish processional march, of sorts, this brisk walk-dance was overseen bythe hosting aristocracy at high-society events.

Mazurka: originating as a waltz-based song and dance in Mazovia, a chorus of men stamped their feet on unexpected beats and improvised complex dance steps.

Nocturne: a piece of reflective music, characterized by the mood of the night, perhaps even of clandestine love.

15

Johannes Brahms

THE LAST OF THE FIRST ROMANTICS

1833-1897

BIOGRAPHY

Johannes Brahms was born into a poor-but-happy German family and grew rapidly in his musical skill under a handful of kind-spirited teachers. One of his teachers saw such promise in the young Brahms that he took him on as a student at no charge.

Brahms began his career playing in night clubs and community choirs (for which he arranged folk songs) and eventually progressed to his own sponsored performances. He sent his own compositions to the renowned critic Robert Schumann and they were returned unopened. This did not stop Brahms, who then hiked 75 miles to Schumann's home to ensure they were reviewed. Schumann's critical review opened "This young eagle is surely going to soar."

His later works were mired in the question: "what is Brahms?" While Brahms's early music followed the passion and exploration of Beethoven, his music became more introspective and less flashy (this is in the age of Wagner and Massenet — flocks of geese and of elephants were storming stages). Brahms was labelled a "Traditionalist," rather than a "Progressivist," like Liszt and Wagner. This led to a rapid deterioration of Brahms's popularity as the next wave of composers took over the reins.

Brahms's later life was filled to the brim with performances of his own works, especially as a pianist and conductor, and with his (possibly romantic) friendship with his late teacher's widow, Clara Schumann

ETHNOMUSICOLOGIST

Brahms's early career provided him with an intimate view on German folk music, which would remain an influence on his writings throughout this life. Many of his most famous songs are arrangements of popular folk songs (such as his entire collections of Volkslieder). Chief among these are "Wiegenlied (Lullaby)," "Sonntag (Sunday)," and "Schwesterlein (Sister, Mine)."

Similarly, between Brahms's early career and his later international career, Brahms toured Europe with a group of Hungarian musicians, most notably Edouard Reményi, whose fierce, stylized violin playing shaped Brahms's view of Hungarian folk msuic and influenced dozens of his most famous compositions. Pieces influenced by Hungarian music include the *Zigeunerlieder* (Gypsy Songs) and the *Hungarian Dances* (Nos. 1-21).

Brahms always cited these as folk songs and arranged them according to his own tastes on the piano; this should not be considered plagiarism, but preservation of German and Hungarian culture.

SYMPHONY NO. 1 IN C MINOR

Brahms's first symphony, first performed when he was already 43 years old, was a late addition to his works. While Brahms's early folk music career delayed his start as a classical composer, still more haltering was the effect of Schumann's prediction that Brahms would be the composer to take over the mantle of Beethoven. Brahms ruminated on the content of *Symphony No. 1* for nearly a decade before it was premiered. While other composers questioned the audacity of writing new symphonies in a post-Beethoven world, Brahms attempted to do nothing more than continue Beethoven's dominance in the sphere.

While *Symphony No. 1* did cement Brahms's legacy and popularity in his day, it also confirmed his role as successor to Beethoven — perhaps overmuch. Early critiques of the symphony labelled it as a contrived work; it was said to be a copy of Beethoven's *Symphony No. 5*, and in fact, the similarities are great.

Beethoven's work opens with a simple theme in C minor, drives it home with heavy motivic repetition, begins a long development section, gives a false recapitulation, and never fully restates the exposition before finishing. While Brahms changes the theme of the symphony, he retains all other features — it is a formal copy of Beethoven's "Fate," down to the oboe solos and the key in which it is written — C minor. Nevertheless, it remains a highly influential and important work in Brahms's output.

EIN DEUTSCHES REQUIEM

One of Brahms's most enduring works is his *Ein Deutsches Requiem*, a choral-orchestral work truly written for the people. While much of Brahms's career was spent paying tribute to folk music — music of the people —Brahms's *Requiem* provides something of a capstone for this philosophy.

Typically, the Requiem Mass is a Latin text sung for funeral services in the Catholic church and has been set by almost every major composer, with a wide variety of interpretations and settings. Brahms's setting of the Requiem text is unique for multiple reasons.

First, his setting is intended to be a liturgical piece for religious members of all stripes, so long as they are German. It is intended to be a mass for the people: it is, truly, A German Requiem (the translation of *Ein Deutsches Requiem*). Germany, often called the seed bed of the

Protestant Reformation, was not particularly concerned with Catholic theology, but in writing a German version of the Requiem, Brahms invites all people of Germany to revel in God, even in the face of death.

Second, Brahms's musical setting is of a different stripe than that of other composers. Mozart's Requiem is filled with the terror of the "Dies Irae," as is Verdi's (with its famous repetition of the theme). Brahms's work is much shorter than the other settings, and is concerned not with the wrath of God, but the compassionate heart of God. Perhaps the most famous excerpt from the work is Movement IV, "Wie lieblich sind deine Wohnungen (How Lovely is Thy Dwelling Place)." Brahms masterfully weaves longing, beauty, and gentleness into his anticipation of the glories of Heaven.

16

Franz Liszt

ROCK STAR OF THE ROMANTICS

1811-1886

BIOGRAPHY

Ferenc (pronounced fair'-ents) Liszt was born to a Hungarian family in the Austrian empire to a political official serving Nicolas Esterhazy (the brother of the crown prince Josef Haydn had served just decades earlier). Liszt's father was his first piano teacher and inspired Liszt's love for religious and Hungarian music.

Liszt's early career, composing at performing by the age of nine, led him to study in Vienna with Carl Czerny (a famous pedagogue and a student of Beethoven) and with Salieri. After his father's death, he returned to Paris, where he attempted a career of teaching and composing, with periods of inactivity. Between 1830 and 1832, he met Berlioz, Paganini, and Chopin, each of whom had significant impact on his own musical style. Liszt's transcriptions of their works (as well as those of Schubert's songs) spread their popularity and dispelled their popular neglect.

Liszt's greatest contributions include the development of the genre of symphonic poem or tone poem, an orchestral work that musically develops the narrative idea of an extramusical concept; his numerous virtuosic piano works; and his elevation of the role of artist from "servant of society" to "pillar of society." Liszt's incredibly complex works and mastery of the piano leave behind a legacy of excellence today.

LISZTOMANIA AND THE PIANO

One of the major influences of Paganini upon the career of Liszt was the concept of virtuosity as a hallmark of the Romantic musician. He is quoted as saying, "What wonderful things might be done with the piano if its technical possibilities were developed as those of the violin have been by Paganini." Liszt adopted the diabolical rumors of Paganini and took them to himself, despite his religious upbringing (and later, religious service). Along with his extraordinary, piano-breaking performances, this reputation drew vast crowds and fanatical audiences, often referred to as "Lisztomania."

In Liszt's day, the traditional placement of the piano in a recital mirrored the placement of the piano in an orchestral performance. Typically, the conductor was also the pianist (or harpsichordist in previous generations) and faced the orchestra, with their back and the keyboard toward the audience. Liszt's public image was largely informed by his dashing good looks, which included the fame of his handsome profile. Because Liszt wished to emphasize his profile and good looks, he turned the piano sideways, the position in which it is generally placed.

Another crucial development of the piano under Liszt was the use of the metal soundboard (the frame to which the strings are attached). Up to Liszt's day, the soundboard was made of wood, but Liszt's powerful and incredibly fast piano playing left soundboards in tattered. On at least one occasion, he is reported to have shattered the soundboard of a piano and certainly broke strings during performances, to great acclaim. Women and critics alike swooned after performances, such was the adoration of his fans.

HUNGARIAN RHAPSODY NO. 2

Liszt's Hungarian heritage was a difficult factor to manage. Initially, he was not admitted to the Paris Conservatoire based on the fact that he was a foreigner. Liszt's father changed the family name from List (pronounced "Lisht," a name of obviously Hungarian origin) to Liszt (pronounced "List," due to the added "z") in order to make his family name more acceptable in the Austrian Empire. The composer himself had to change his name from Ferenc to Franz in order to legitimize his position in artistic society.

Nevertheless, many of Liszt's works draw on his Hungarian heritage. Along with Brahms, Liszt took musical refuge in the nationalistic movement sweeping across Europe that treasured Hungarian music, with its harmonic minor keys and seemingly spontaneous accents. Liszt made this clear in a number of songs and other musical works, but perhaps the most famous example is in his "Hungarian Rhapsodies," numbering 19 piano solos. Number Two is perhaps most well-known for its use in both Bugs Bunny and Tom and Jerry cartoons, which left Liszt's mark on popular culture.

Liszt's overall technique for playing was a dramatic departure from those of previous generations of pianists. Czerny and Beethoven were largely concerned with proper posture (forward on the piano bench) and hand-only playing (emphasizing the role of the hand and fingers), whereas Liszt felt he could not adequately artistically express his music when forced to carry his body in this way. Instead, Liszt developed a manner of playing that heavily emphasized the arm and the movement of the wrist, which allowed him to playing with greater strength and precise accentuation. Where other pianists were concerned with delicate expression, Liszt's thrown-back head and full-bodied playing created a craze over this new and "more complete" artistic expression. These are employed to great effect in the Hungarian Rhapsodies.

Rhapsody No. 2 is Liszt's highly dramatic *czárdás* (a Hungarian dance comprising alternating fast and slow sections) in C# minor. Among Liszt's pianistic pyrotechnics included in the work is the crossover technique in which the left hand crosses over the right hand to continue long sweeping passagework. Common for modern pianists and even relatively simple pieces in today's music, the technique astounded audiences in Liszt's day, giving it the name the "Three-Hand Technique."

The themes of *Rhapsody No. 2* develop, ironically, a Romanian musical theme (closely associated with the Roma people group, who occupied parts of Hungary, as well). The piece begins with a short prelude and moves into its recognizable slow-movement theme. Where many *czárdás* selections have a rather sudden transition to the faster portion, Liszt allows the embellishments to pick up speed as he transitions the work to its fast portion. Liszt's exploration of the extremes of pitch abd tempo heightens the Roma folk music feel, while also bringing a quality of artistic expression to the stylized folk music.

In addition to the other showy techniques included in the work, Liszt also depends on one more development to the piano during his lifetime. *Rhapsody No. 2* depends frequently on notes repeated in quick succession, which would not have been possible before Liszt's time. Liszt had a lifelong relationship with Erard Piano Company, which was responsible for adding the pedals to the foot of the piano and for the double-escapement action, which quickly catches the hammer and repositions it to strike the strings again. Prior piano mechanisms were prone to catching and took longer to reset, which would have prevent Lisztian-style playing and compositions from ever meeting audiences. Liszt's goal to be the Paganini of the piano was realized in his lifetime.

17

Hector Berlioz

THE ROMANTIC COLOR

1803-1869

BIOGRAPHY

Like many French youth during the Napoleonic Wars, Berlioz was educated at home, as many educators were drafted into the French military. His home education gave him great freedom to explore his own interests, which included pursuing studying music with instrumental ensembles.

Because his music education was informal and hands-on, Berlioz knew no limits to his creativity. Where other composers learned compositional and orchestration (how to employ the instruments of the orchestra together) rules from a teacher or their teacher's work, Berlioz discovered each instrument at the hands of the musicians who played them. This allowed him to write using innovative techniques for each instrument — techniques that sometimes arose from happenstance or knoodling, but to which he was nevertheless exposed as a young composer.

Berlioz went on to receive the *Prix de Rome* (Rome Prize) and began an international career in composing and conducting. After this, he wrote the first widely circulated orchestration textbook and traveled across Europe teaching others to wrote in his new dramatically expressive manner. While his writing style was considered unconventional in his day, his orchestral techniques inspire even modern composers. The impact of his work can be felt particularly in necessarily-dramatic fields, such as film and entertainment music.

The anecdotes of Berlioz's mental instability are often comical, if not alarming, and provide excellent fodder for discussion of the role of virtue and moderation in daily life.

BERLIOZ'S MUSE

At the beginning of the Nineteenth Century, the works of Shakespeare were just beginning to be translated into other languages so foreign audiences could enjoy the appeal of the Great Bard. This would have great impact on classical music, as composers like Berlioz and Verdi flocked to these dramatically expressive works. Berlioz saw a performance of *Hamlet* in Paris and was enamoured with the Ophelia, an Irish actress by the name of Harriet Smithson. He immediately fell in love with her and pursued her feverishly for a few years, writing letters and requesting to meet her throughout much of that time. He even rented an apartment near hers for some time, just to make sure he saw her, though she refused ever to meet him.

Smithson finally attended a performance of *Lélio*, the sequel to *Symphonie Fantastique*. After attending, she sent a letter to Berlioz, congratulating him for his work and fame and thanking him for dedicating the works to her (a frightening thought for the educated listener).

They then began a short affair and a longer marriage, ended by her career's decline and subsequent alcoholism. After her death in 1853, he remarried to the opera singer with whom he was having an affair. After Berlioz's death, Smithson's body was exhumed and reburied next to his, fulfilling one of the enigmatic composer's life's wishes.

SYMPHONIE FANTASTIQUE

It is in *Symphonie Fantastique* that Berlioz's compositional and dramatic skills come to a head. With his devotion to Shakespeare, exploration of the orchestra, and obsession with Smithson; Berlioz was poised to create a wildly dramatic and innovative work that is now known as the first Romantic symphony.

For a complete translation of Berlioz's program notes for the original performance, please see Appendix D. Here, Berlioz provides the story for each movement, which gives greater insight into the ingenuity of the orchestration.

The symphony as a whole is centered on a recurring theme known as the *ideé fixe*, or "fixed idea," akin to that of an "earworm" or, more simply, an idea you cannot shake from your head. Berlioz's use of this theme throughout the work is crucial for understanding the dramatic narrative, but it is perhaps his alterations of the *ideé fixe* that are most intriguing, including the glimpse of it before the artist is beheaded in Movement IV and the "diabolical fest" in Movement V.

Some of the novel implementations of the orchestra include the ballroom music in Movement II and the sudden freeze of time when the *ideé fixe* occurs; the isolation and sparse pastoral instrumentation in Movement III; the use of woodwinds to imitate the scorning crowd in Movement IV; and the cacophony of instruments in Movement V: the bells toll midnight, the sacred trombones blare the "Dies Irae" chant, the strings murmur the breeze. Rather than demonstrate the audience's emotions, Berlioz makes the listeners feel them instead.

18

Giuseppe Verdi

THE ROMANTIC DRAMATIST

1813-1901

BIOGRAPHY

Giuseppe Verdi was born to a middle class family in Italy in the early part of the Romantic era. Early on, Giuseppe was training to be a priest in the Roman Catholic church until a culminating experience redirected his passions. He was bringing the elements of the Eucharist forward to the priest during a Mass when he heard the organ for the first time. Pausing, transfixed, he remained in a trance-like state until the priest had vainly called for his attention multiple times, at which point the priest struck him in the face and he fell down the altar steps. Verdi awoke with a diminished view of the Church and an exalted view of music. He never abandoned God, but did not view institutional religion as a necessity.

Verdi's career spanned decades and was transformative to the Italian musical landscape. His earlier works are written in a quasi-Classical style, highly dependent on form and traditional narrative arcs, but his middling works become more exploratory. Most of his compositions are in the operatic realm, with some art songs and the occassional instrumental work. Here, his admiration of Shakespeare (whom he lovingly referred to as "Papa") comes into full view, as Shakespeare's works are dramatically excellent, with the music always serving the purpose of the story.

Verdi is remembered as the great storyteller of the Romantic era for the legacy of his twenty-eight operas.

RISORGIMENTO HERO

The nineteenth century was a vital century for the progress of democracy and independence, begun with America's War for Independence and continuing in France and spreading through the rest of Europe. Italy was also a part of this spreading movement and drove out the Austrian influence. The movement for independence, however, was somewhat underground. Verdi's music incorporated secret messages in support of the Resurgence Movement (in Italian, "Risorgimento"), particularly the opening chorus of Aida, in which a chorus of Hebrew slaves sings about returning to their homeland and out of captivity. The refrain of this chorus became something of a theme song, whistled in the streets of Italy by supporters of the movement.

Verdi's name also became a rallying cry for the Risorgimento movement. Not only was he an underground supporter of Italian independence, his name also summed up the support for the military general-become-leader, Victor Emmanuel II, with people crying out "Viva Verdi" wherever they went:

Viva	Long live
Emmanuel	Victor Emmanuel
Rei	King
Di	of
Italia	Italy

MESSA DA REQUIEM

Perhaps Verdi's most popular (and most-referenced) work is his *Messa da Requiem*, or *Requiem*. The Requiem Mass is the Mass service with the accompanying texts for a funeral. It is a Mass for the dead. Many of the greatest composers have set the Requiem Mass to music and dedicated them to patrons, or have been commissioned to write them for wealthy patrons.

Verdi's composition came about differently. Verdi felt that a great tribute was due to Rossini upon his death, and he suggested to his publisher that each of the greatest composers in Italy write and submit a movement for a collective *Requiem Mass* in his honor. After a year, the project was not yet completed and was shelved until Alessandro Manzoni died. Manzoni was a great novelist and poet who helped codify the forms of Italian poetry (which made libretto-writing and vocal composing easier) and Verdi picked up the score once more and completed the work.

Like Brahms, Verdi's *Requiem* reflects his own view of God, though Verdi's is more negative. Verdi's *Requiem* frequently repeats the musical motif of the "Dies Irae," the text which explains the acts that will take place on the Day of God's Wrath — Judgement Day. It is a popular theme and has often been employed in popular culture to accompany moments of dramatic terror.

The work was premiered on the first anniversary of Manzoni's death and was repeated dozens of times in the following months. Critical receptions was poor, as many thought the work "too theatrical" for a sacred work. This was a common criticism of many popular composers, but for Verdi's *Requiem*, the critique almost rings too true. Now, the *Requiem* is often referred to as "Verdi's Greatest Opera" or "Verdi's Church Opera," as it is overwhelmingly dramatic. Each of the four soloists plays a an important role in conveying the desperation of the soul at the hour of death, and the interplay between the soprano soloist and the chorus in the final movement, "Libera me," is nothing short of operatic grandeur and intimacy.

The "Offertorio" is a stunning vocal quartet that grounds the otherwise metaphysical work with the reminder that the *Requiem Mass* is still a piece of sacred, church music. Additionally, lest anyone think that Verdi's greatness resides only in his passionate, Romantic-era compositional prowess, the "Sanctus" is a highly complex double fugue that reminds the audience of Verdi's original inspiration for music: the church organ.

19

Richard Wagner

THE ROMANTIC *AUTEUR*

1813-1883

BIOGRAPHY

Richard Wagner was born to a single mother and never knew his father. A child passionate about learning and studying, he drank deeply of the folk lore of his native Germany and of Scandinavian culture. He also frequently wrote his own stories and music, even as a child. He was dismissed early from piano lessons — he teacher assessed that he was ill equipped to do well and would not make a professional musician.

As Wagner grew, he became something of an idiomatic musician and personality. His early music was fairly well-received, with his first opera, Rienzi, is still excerpted today. However, his political writings earned him expulsion from Germany and it was many years before his reputation permitted him to return.

Many of his works are based on the legends he enjoyed as a child, though re-arranged or re-formatted to suit his own dramatic and ideological purposes. His legacy is tainted by this fact. Wagner was part of a growing anti-Semitic movement in his own day, and his music was employed by the Nazi regime during World War II as a means of nationalist propaganda.

Wagner's legacy is a difficult one to judge without reservation, but his music can and ought to be considered in its own right as a work of exceptional dramatic brilliance.

GESAMTKUNSTWERK

One of Wagner's most influential ideas was the concept of the *gesamptkunstwerk.* Typically translated "total work of art," it might be better translated as "a work of total art." Wagner considered opera to be the queen of the arts — the sum total of all artistic endeavors serving a narrative. Dramatic (narrative, poetry, acting), visual (costume, set, and light design), musical (vocal, orchestral) arts were all used in the making of opera; if any of these were out of accord with the others in serving the story, Wagner considered this an underachievement of opera's potential.

Wagner, then, sought to control every aspect of opera in order to tell a story as comprehensively and as well as one possibly could. Wagner was the first, and remains one of the only, composer to write his own libretto for every opera he wrote (a staggering thirteen, considering most of them are between 3 and 5 hours). He developed the stage designs and costume designs alongside visual artists. He even constructed his own theatre in Bayreuth, for the purpose of immersing the audience in the storytelling. The technical aspects of the theatre were hidden, the lights were dimmed, and orchestra was out of view of the audience; these not only made the performance more immersive, but gave the sense that the music was so tightly linked to the drama that the orchestral music simply arose out of the story playing out on stage. These concepts inform the design of modern movie theaters.

Wagner's works are polarizing. Many love them; many hate them; few are neutral regarding his works. But it is certain that he accomplished what he desired: a cohesive, unified dramatic experience.

PARSIFAL

Wagner's crowning achievement was an opera he spent decades preparing for. Born out of his love for Arthurian legend, *Parsifal* tells the story of a Pure Fool (the translation of "Parsi-fal") made wise by compassion. *Parsifal* follows the story of a young knight (Parsifal) of the Holy Grail who passes the test to remain "pure" and retrieves the Holy Spear from the land of the sorcerer Klingsor. By returning to the Grail Knights with the Holy Spear and righting the wrongs of the Grail Knights, the world is reborn in purity on Good Friday.

The story unfolds over nearly five hours and it is replete with spiritual and pseudo-spiritual imagery (some Christian, some Buddhist, some unique to Wagner's ideology) and many important narrative themes. What makes understanding the flow of the opera possible are the many *leitmotifs* Wagner uses to unify the work.

Leitmotifs are recurring musical ideas that relate to a dramatic concept (a person, place, object, or idea). They range in length from just a few notes or chords to long passages of 30 seconds or more. *Leitmotifs* are easily understood by modern audiences as they have become the fundamental building blocks of storytelling in film (especially in the soundtracks of John Williams, a student of classical music, in his scores for *Jaws*, *Indiana Jones*, *Harry Potter*, and especially the *Star Wars* franchise).

It is not always clear why certain themes are associated with certain characters, but Wagner clearly demarcated their presence in his manuscripts and scores. *Leitmotifs* can also interact with one another and be transformed, so understanding every allusion and interpretation takes a very attentive ear or a full score of the music. Regardless of your level of awareness, the *leitmotifs* do their job and communicate rich dramatic information without ever saying a word.

20

Giaccomo Puccini

THE ROMANTIC REALIST

1858-1924

BIOGRAPHY

Giacomo Puccini was born in Italy to a family with a great musical lineage: the patriarchs of the family had served as *maestri di cappella* ("master of the chapel," or music director) for 120 years by the time the boy was born. When he was only six, his father died and the position of cathedral organist was held for Giacomo until he came of age with musical training.

Puccini grew up in the wake of Verdi and Wagner and the emphasis on music-dramas. As Italy's literature shifted, the dominating movement in art was *verismo* (realism), which valued the portrayal of the full range and depth of human life. Puccini's emotional musical portrayals (particularly those of female protagonists) would be a driving force for the continued success of opera.

Puccini became widely recognized a leader in opera for a number of reasons, but Puccini's accurate portrayals of the common man and his struggles against social conventions and his own psychology (which had typically been reserved for the noble heroes in previous eras of storytelling) brought him popular renowned.

Puccini's operas remain the most well-known portion of his output, and rightly so: his excellent use of the orchestra and libretto to convey drama made him the Wagner of the common man's art, even to this day.

PUCCINI AND THE RECORDING ARTS

At the turn of the century, Puccini was coming into his own as a musical artist, just as technology was coming into its own with the boom of the Industrial Revolution. Vinyl records were becoming an installation in wealthier homes, trickling down into the homes of the people as prosperity spread.

Recording technology was at its earliest stages, but advances were coming quickly and Puccini frequently took advantage of these technological shifts. A brief survey of earlier operas shows that many arias (operatic solos) lasted between six and nine minutes — a duration appropriate for watching drama unfold on the stage, but not appropriate for the new and improved stage: the phonograph in the parlor.

Puccini recognized this dramatic shift and the potential for an increased audience (and thus, increased popularity, record sales, and ticket sales) and wrote his arias accordingly. The average length of a Puccini aria is approximately four minutes, which is the length of play of a single side of a vinyl record.

Similarly, many of the opera artists of the age who desired to sell records began to adopt Puccini arias as their "big hits," allowing them to record brief, powerful numbers and bring them to mass audiences. Dozens of opera stars catapulted into the spotlight and into the sitting room; they are still remembered as the earliest and greatest of singers and held in high esteem, all because of Puccini's innovative marketing tactic.

LA BOHÈME

While Puccini's operatic works include a large number of "greatest hits," including *Manon Lescaut*, *Tosca*, *Madama Butterfly*, *Il Trittico*, and *Turandot*; Puccini's enduring legacy resides in his most frequently performed opera: *La Bohème*.

La Bohème tells the story of young citizens of Paris living through a period of desperate poverty and a particularly cold winter. Rodolfo is a struggling young writer who shares a room with one of his struggling artist companions. On their way out to drinks one night, Rodolfo is left by his friends and is met by a woman from down the hall, Mimi. He invites her, agreeing to light the extinguished candle she is carrying for warmth and light (a hopeful cure for her fits of coughing). They quickly introduce themselves to one another and confess their mutual love.

Catching up to Rodolfo's friends at the cafe, the two learn more of each other and the rowdy gang of youths who live the life of the struggling artist, referred to in French as the *vie de bohème* ("Bohemian life"). Weeks later, Mimi stumbles up to Rodolfo's roommate and seeks his advice regarding Rodolfo's jealousy. She discovers that Rodolfo is not coldly jealous, but concerned that Mimi's coughing fits are a sign that she is dying of consumption and that the couple must not have much time remaining to enjoy one another. They quarrel and depart estranged.

Several months later, the gang of young men is enjoying a small amount of success and joviality when they are interrupted with a message that Mimi is outside, struggling through her final moments of life, and wishes to spend her dying breath with Rodolfo, who welcomes her in with open arms while the others try to pawn their few belongings to purchase medicine for Mimi. The couple reminisce together, drifting off into what is discovered to be fantasy for him and death for her.

Some of the most stunning moments of the opera are the moments of insight into genuine human struggles — struggles that did not often appear in opera prior to the *verismo* movement. The famous scene "Che gelida manina (How cold are your hands)" in which the two are introduced provides a classic example of Puccini's orchestration, vocal writing, and reasons for his popular appeal (including the hasty confession of love found in too many operas). The final scene, in which the heroine dies of consumption (tuberculosis), is reminiscent of Verdi's La Traviata, but only because of subject matter. Where Verdi's heroine dies in a fit of ecstatic memory and disconsolation, Mimi meets her last breath with an intimate whimper; Verdi's is a death fit for the stage, Puccini's for the living room.

Students will find Puccini's thematic repetition and use of melody to be memorable and emotionally sensitive and find the story easy to follow and likely easy to understand, especially as Puccini's opera was almost exactly duplicated in the long-running and award-winning Broadway musical *Rent*, in which the poor New York inhabitants are dying of AIDS, rather than tuberculosis. Puccini's masterfully crafted opera has staying power, and a brilliant exposition of love.

IV

Nationalism

THE MOVEMENT OF DEMOCRACY

CA. 1800-1900

21

Introduction

NATIONALISM CHARACTERISTICS

As Europe entered the 1800s, democratic ideals became the center of political dialogue. The Revolutions in American and France paved the way for equality among political and social classes and removed the previous ruling elites from their places of power. Combining these influences with growing senses of national identity in places like Germany, Italy, Bohemia (Czech Republic), Norway, Finland, and America; nationalism became another predominating factor, alongside Romanticism, in the nineteenth century.

While the nationalistic movements looked and sounded different in each country, there are through-lines which can be traced across the century. In most cases, there is an emphasis on the common man and his folk stories, folk songs, and folk dances; there is a unification of language and national or ethnic identity. There is also a deterioration of the historical concept that each country comprises one nation, as political borders become rigid boundary lines and cultures solidify in this era.

A NOTE ON NATIONALISM

One helpful distinction to make is that America is not always a helpful starting point in these conversations. A country is loosely defined as a geographic region with political borders. A nation, on the other hand, is a group of people with a shared culture. As "The Great Melting Pot," the country of America is made up not of one nation, but many nations with many cultures that have, over time, melted into a strange conglomeration of traditions.

While it can certainly be said that there is such an entity as "American popular culture," there are immense regional differences on both the macro- and the micro-level. The food, song, and celebrations of the American South are not aligned with those in the Pacific Northwest or those in New England. Even the cultural traditions of the various boroughs and neighborhoods of New York City provide a case study in variety.

Historically, though, the political boundaries of a nation or empire were not so rigid; the country extended as far as the people who loosely shared its culture — no more, no less. Students should be encouraged to adopt this historical mindset and framework as their study moves into an early modern era with its associated political and cultural struggles.

ETHNOMUSICOLOGY

While musicology is the study of music history, ethnomusicology is the study of the music of a people group. In its earliest form, ethnomusicology was often concerned with collecting and anthologizing folk songs and dances throughout the world before they were subsumed by modern cultural ideals. Early names in this work include Roud, Vaughan-Williams, Bartok, and Butterfield.

Ethnomusicologists have developed various means of preserving cultural music, which can largely be categorized into three avenues of work:

Gatherers: Collect and anthologize folk songs and dances for historical preservation.

Arrangers: Preserve folk music by converting it into art music for continued performance.

Reflectors: Preserve a national musical style by incorporating its elements into newly-composed music.

MAJOR COMPOSERS

Grieg (Norway)

Edvard Grieg (1843-1907) was a member of the leading generation of Norwegian nationalists. His music led the way in capturing Norwegian cultural sentiments and inspired generations of composers of Scandinavian music. His friendships with Liszt and with Henrik Ibsen shaped his music and the subjects of his works. His most famous piece is the *Peer Gynt Suites*.

Tchaikovsky (Russia)

Peter Ilyich Tchaikovsky (alternatively Chaikoffsky, Chaikobski, Tchaikoffski, etc.) (1840-1893) was a highly influential Russian composer. Initially spurned for his "too-European-sounding" music, his orchestral innovations shaped the coming generations of Russian composers. His operas, art songs, and orchestral works reflected Russian literary and historical heritage. Perhaps his most famous work was his least favorite: The *1812 Overture*. Additional influential Russian nationalistic works include Modest Mussorgsky's *Boris Gudonov* and Igor Stravinsky's *Firebird Suite*.

Vaughan Williams (England)

Ralph Vaughan Williams (1872-1958) was an English composer of the first generation of ethnomusicologists. A student of Charles Villiers Stanford and later a professor at the Royal College of Music, Vaughan

Williams played an active role in bringing English folk music to the world and reinvigorating English church music through his rich arrangements. Many of his works are mainstays of the repertoire, but his most well known may be *The Lark Ascending*.

Jean Sibelius (Finland)

Johan Julius Christian Sibelius (1865-1957) was renowned as a Finnish nationalist composer, primarily for his symphonic poems reflective of the landscape. His later works, especially his symphonies, identified him as a composer worthy of the classical canon. His most impactful work came in his political protest work, *Symphony No. 5*, "Finland Awakes," now known as *Finlandia*.

Dvorak (Bohemia/America)

Antonín Dvorak (1841-1904) was a student of Bedrich Smetana and became the most famous Czech composer of his day. His international reputation led him to New York, where he led a school of music and travelled America, whose folk songs shaped his compositions. His career-defining Czech work was the *Slavonic Dances*, though the *Symphony No. 9* "For a New World" holds his place in the canon. Additional influential Russian nationalistic works include: Bedrich Smetana's "Die Moldau" from *Ma Vlast*.

Copland

Aaron Copland (1900-1990) was the first American student of the influential French pedagogue and composer Nadia Boulanger. His earliest (and latest) works were firmly set in the classical mindset of the time, shaped by jazz, neoclassicism, and serialism. As he grew in popularity among composers, he recognized the need to write for the musical public, after which point his most enduring works were written. These were almost entirely based on American folk traditions and his work in this arena shaped the "American sound" such as is found in *Appalachian Spring*.

22

Edvard Grieg

THE COMPOSER OF MAGIC

1843-1907

BIOGRAPHY

Edvard Grieg was born and raised in Norway to a family of musicians. His mother was a pianist and an able teacher, raising Edvard up as a pianist from the age of six.

Grieg went on to study at the Leipzig Conservatory, an experience he felt did not enrich him musically. He acknowledged his growth in skill, but complained that he learned nothing of how to musically express himself.

This latter goal was achieved when he travelled to Denmark in the 1860s. In Copenhagen, he met an eclectic group of Norwegian authors, poets, and composers who introduced him to the Norwegian national style. (One of these, Rikard Nordraak, was the composer of the Norwegian national anthem and became a close friend of Grieg during his stay in Denmark.)

Grieg later traveled to Rome, where he worked with Franz Liszt.

Liszt's performances and promotion of Grieg's work helped to spread his name across the continent, where he would later be engaged in touring for piano and orchestral performances for the remainder of his career.

Grieg's bent toward nationalistic music captivated him for the rest of his life, inspiring countless art songs and lyrical piano works. His wife (and first cousin) Nina Hagerup was a faithful interpreter of his music beyond his lifetime. He remains an iconic figure in Norwegian music and concerts can still be heard at his home in Bergen.

NORWEGIAN NATIONALISM

The unique cultural heritage of many Scandinavian cultures is frequently tied to their stories. Students are likely familiar with these Nordic stories — the myths of the Norse gods and their many misadventures. While these came to their present form because of the Christian influence on Scandinavia in the early Middle Ages, this influence was only possible because of the belief in the supernatural that was already in place in the region.

Supernaturalism is simply a belief in the supernatural. It can be loosely characterized by a belief that the uncanny can be explained by the supernatural or that there is a melding of the natural and supernatural worlds. These are common features of Norse and Scandinavian folklore. The first can be seen worldwide in the belief of cryptids — supernatural creatures used to explain strange-but-natural phenomena, like Bigfoot. The latter is more common in longer storytelling, in which supernatural creatures (like elves, dwarves, or trolls) have an influence on the goings-on of the world of natural man. Consider enjoying examples of this by reading a Scandinavian folk tale. One common, and perhaps familiar, story is "East of the Sun and West of the Moon," though Scandinavian folk tales are many and thoroughly enjoyable! Grieg's *Lyrical Pieces* for piano capture many of these stories and sentiments beautifully.

THE *PEER GYNT SUITES*

As Norway's nationalistic music is rooted in supernaturalism, it is important to understand how understand how Grieg conveys this in his music. In a wide variety of Grieg's pieces inspired by supernaturalism, Grieg relies heavily on contrast and the use of extremes to convey a sense of the supernatural.

The *Peer Gynt Suite* is a highly nationalistic work. The music Grieg wrote was originally incidental music for a play by Henrik Ibsen, the famous Norwegian playwright. Ibsen collected and codified the story of Peer Gynt, a subversive folk antihero common to stories in the region. Unlike many folk heros, Peer demonstrates moral living by giving a negative example.

Peer Gynt is a care-free and fame-seeking young man who sets out to find adventure and success. His poor choices constantly put him on paths to ruin, which he often narrowly escapes. By the end of the story, he returns from traveling the world, destitute and alone. He is redeemed, though, by the love of the faithful Solveig, who has awaited his arrival through the long years. Her love rehabilitates him and they spend their remaining years happy together.

Two of the works are exceptionally well-known and employ the use of extremes alongside an increasing chromaticism to convey a sense of the supernatural. The most well-known of these works are "Morning Mood" and "In the Hall of the Mountain King," which employ these high contrasts of pitch, dynamics, and tempo to exciting dramatic effect.

Less well-known, but stunningly beautiful is "Solveig's Song," the homecoming song sung by Peer's faithful bride-to-be. It appears in both instrumental and vocal versions. A close analysis of this piece shows both the supernatural influence and the folk influence with which Grieg infuses the song. In the opening section, Solveig's melody (which is based on the character's theme from the "Prelude" of *Suite No. 1*) is highly chromatic, emphasizing her inner turmoil while she watches Peer struggle through life. This initial melody is in a minor mode, whereas her reminiscing daydream ("La la la") is in the major mode and in a much faster tempo, dwelling longer on high notes as she drifts into the happy thought of her future with Peer.

23

Peter Ilyich Tchaikovsky

THE COMPOSER-HISTORIAN

1840-1893

BIOGRAPHY

Tchaikovsky grew up in the late ages of Tsarist Russia when the formerly rigid boundaries between Europe and the Russian empire were dissolving, with artistic culture as the main exports and imports.

Tchaikovsky began music at a young age, composing his first work at the age of five. His musical career was stunted, though, as there was no conservatory in the Russian empire at the time. Instead, he studied law and served as a clerk for several years before leaving that career and traveling across Europe to study the music of other musical hotspots.

After two years in Europe, Tchaikovsky returned home and became one of the first students and graduates of the St. Petersburg Conservatory. His music was highly influenced by his time in Europe and his attempts at popular music were spurned by other composers who deigned his music "not Russian enough." This was countered by the people's opinion, which held Tchaikovsky's music in high regard, especially his three famous ballets: *The Sleeping Beauty*, *The Nutcracker*, and *Swan Lake*.

Ultimately, while Tchaikovsky's music helped spark the unique Russian sound that would develop after him. Though not particularly nationalistic in its sound (for his day), Tchaikovsky's content is often focused on Russian nationalistic elements -- poetry (in his art songs), literature (as in his opera, *Eugene Onegin*), folk tales and literary folk tales (as in the ballets), and his symphonic works (as in the *1812 Overture*).

RUSSIAN NATIONALISM

There is a long tradition of the connection between Russian history and Russian music. The tradition is heightened in the 1800s by Romantic-era nationalistic composers like Mussorgsky (in *Boris Gudonov*), Borodin, Glazunov, and Rimsky-Korsakov (in *Prince Igor*), and Prokofiev (in *War and Peace*). Interest in Russian historical (and mythological) characters was a major focus in opera and in the popular mind.

One major historical battle that gave strength to the Russian nationalistic movement was found in the Napoleonic Wars — the Battle of Borodino. Borodino was the final battle fought between the French and the Russians before the French infiltrated Moscow. Napolean's last major campaign began in the summer of 1812 and ended later that year.

Borodino remains one of the bloodiest days in military history, with over 100,000 casualties in a single day. Though the French won, they suffered major casualties and could not keep momentum in capturing Moscow and were chased back to France, returning to their home country through the Slavic winter with approximately ten percent of their original forces. It was ultimately a pyrrhic victory for France and an ultimate victory for Russia.

For the Russian people, Borodino was such a symbol of Russian success that Dostoevsky memorialized it in the opening chapters of his famous *War and Peace*.

THE 1812 OVERTURE

In 1882, Tchaikovsky was commissioned to write a musical work celebrating the success of Russia in light of the fairly recent publishing of War and Peace and the 25th anniversary of the coronation of the current tsar. Many festivities were held in 1882 as part of the All-Russia Arts and Industry Exhibition. Tchaikovsky completed the symphonic work in six weeks at the end of 1880. The work was performed at the Cathedral of Christ Our Saviour in Moscow, which was initially constructed out of gratitude to God for delivering Russia in 1812.

The piece is composed largely by stringing together four important nationalistic works:

1) "O Lord, Save Thy People" — a popular Russian Orthodox hymn which serves as the prayer of the Russian people for God's defense in the midst of the military crisis.

2) "Le Marseillaise" — the French national anthem before and after Napolean's reign, including when Tchaikovsky wrote the work. (Napolean had the piece removed as the national anthem during his term as Emperor.)

3) "U Vorot, Vorot" — a Russian folk song singing of mourning and bitterness in the midst of winter.

4) "God Save the Tsar" — the national anthem of Russia when Tchaikovsky wrote the work.

Tchaikovsky weaves together these four works to summarize the events of the Battle of Borodino and the advance of the French all the way through to the Russian victory, celebrated most famously with a unique section of the orchestra: artillery. Sixteen cannon fires are used throughout the overture, along with the cathedral's bells, to celebrate victory.

24

Ralph Vaughan Williams

THE CODIFIER OF ENGLISH MUSIC

1872-1958

BIOGRAPHY

Ralph (pronounced either "Ralph" or "Rafe") was born into an historic Welsh/English family devoted to the public good (many family members were involved in the church or in public law). He was composing at an early age and grew in piano and violin studies with a preference for the latter. He studied at the Royal College of Music with some of the greatest English composers of the previous generation and eventually also studied with Maurice Ravel, which inspired an appreciation for impressionistic musical influences.

Vaughan Williams was part of the initial waves of English ethnomusicology, following in the footsteps of Cecil Sharp and Lucy Broadwood, composers who transcribed the folk songs of the English countryside.

He went on to serve in World War I, losing many younger colleagues and friends in the war (including the celebrated composer George Butterworth). Afterward, he returned to the Royal College of Music to teach and mentor many of the next generation of British composers. His lifelong friendship with Gustav Holst ended with Holst's death in 1934, a severe blow to Ralph.

His enduring works include nine symphonies, numerous symphonic works, operas, art songs, and a great library of choral music which endures in the Anglican tradition as well as in the concert hall.

ENGLISH NATIONALISM

Most music historians note that there are few major composers between Henry Purcell (1659-1695) and Ralph Vaughan Williams; the 17th, 18th, and 19th Centuries passed without another influential English composer.

English nationalistic music is largely reflected in the two sides of Vaughan Williams's career: ethnomusicology and song composing. Much of the reinvention of English music centered on picking up elements of folk music and incorporating them into art music. The use of modes (ancient pitch collections with different whole and half step relationships) and the use of the pentatonic scale became central features in art music that reflected English nationalism.

At the same time, English poetry was in the midst of a revival. The Georgian poets (named after the Greek word for "farmer") redirected popular attention to the English countryside and away from the metropolitan centers of the historic poets of England (who were largely men of upper classes). In particular, A. E. Housman's *A Shropshire Lad* became an incredibly powerful influence upon composers and other poets. The dawn of World War I (then called "The Great War") reminded many in England that the boys going off to war were the common men of England. The everyman, who was protecting the honor of England, became the hero of the new age and he was celebrated by Housman and the Georgian poets.

THE LARK ASCENDING

Based on a poem by George Meredith (the full text of which can be found in Appendix E), *The Lark Ascending* is a violin concerto written in 1914 and first performed in 1920. The original performance in 1920 was for only violin and piano, while the 1921 version of the work is for violin and orchestra. The poem's text describes the flight of a lark, one of the most common songbirds in England, and Vaughan Williams expressively communicates the sentiment of the poem (without using words) through his many musical influences. In the original score, Vaughan Williams quoted only some of the lines:

He rises and begins to round, / He drops the silver chain of sound,
Of many links without a break, / In chirrup, whistle, slur and shake...
For singing till his heaven fills, / 'Tis love of earth that he instils,
And ever winging up and up, / Our valley is his golden cup,
And he the wine which overflows / To lift us with him when he goes...
'Till lost on his aerial rings / In light, and then the fancy sings.

In the opening measures, one can hear the influence of French impressionism on Vaughan Williams, as the strings provide a gentle carpet of sound over which the violin plays, representing both the lark and the lark's flight.

The orchestral accompaniment is largely modal, reflective of Vaughan Williams's preference for historical English folk music; the violin largely plays pentatonic melodies within these modes. The effect is a rather open sound, echoing the open air space above the poem's lark.

The lark begins to sing in short monophonic phrases of slow trills and arced phrases. Eventually, the phrases become longer and longer, until the violin soars as the lark takes flight. Vaughan Williams develops a few small motifs which string together the entire 15 minute work.

25

Jean Sibelius

THE COMPOSER OF INDEPENDENCE

1865-1957

BIOGRAPHY

Johan Sibelius was born to a middle class, musical family in the Grand Duchy of Finland, a then-autonomous member of the Russian Empire. He was brought up in a Swedish-speaking family, but attended the first Finnish-speaking school in the occupied territory.

As he grew, Johan realized an affinity for the violin and for composing, settling in at the Helsinki Music Institute (now the Sibelius Academy). There, he flourished in violin and composing, taking up the great mantel of Romantic nationalism and his "musical name," "Jean." Many of his most well-known and beloved works are based on the Scandinavian epic *Kalevala*, which inspired from him many tone poems, art songs, and choral works, and an opera.

Sibelius's inventive tone poems (or symphonic poems) and symphonies left his mark on the world of classical music. Inspired to some degree by the great Classical era composers, his works build on the art of form and take on new depth through his precise writing. (One piece of advice he left to the following generation was that one should never write an unintentional note in music.)

Sibelius's love of the finer things in life — alcohol and cigars among them — left him in a great amount of debt, which was slightly relieved when, in 1898, he received a perpetual grant from the Finnish government to allow him to write without financial pressure.

Sibelius retired to a relatively quiet life after much success in the public eyes. His final 10 years were spent at his villa (which he named after his wife, Aino) revising his many musical works. The home, Ainola, is now a state museum in his honor.

FINNISH NATIONALISM

Though Finland was, for a time, an independent duchy of Russia, the 1890s saw increasingly strict control exercised by the Russian government. This policy was known as the "Russification of Finland." In that time, Russia exerted dominance in the following spheres:

1. Political — revoking autonomous rule by Finnish subjects.
2. Religious — criminalizing attendance at Lutheran services by Orthodox Catholics.
3. Martial — conscripting the Finnish military into Russian military service and policies.
4. Bureaucratic — restaffing many government offices with Russian officers.

In the midst of this great political upheaval, the Finnish people sought revolution and Sibelius helped to provide this revolution in his own way. It would be several decades before Finland earned their independence, but subtle machinations against the Russian influence helped to bolster support for Finland all across the European continent.

FINLANDIA

Originally written in 1899 as a part of the pieces entitled "Press Celebrations Music," Sibelius's *Finlandia* is likely his most well-known historical and political work. The Press Celebrations were a covert political protest against Russian censorship, hence the celebration of the Finnish press.

The "Press Celebrations Music" was a suite of seven musical works — a prelude followed by six tableaus. Each of the tableaus depicts an important moment of Finnish history:

1. **The Song of Väinämöinen** depicts the creator of the world in the Kalevala singing the universe into being.
2. **The Finns are Baptized by Bishop Henry** depicts the Christianization of Scandinavia.
3. **Scene from Duke Johan's Court** depicts the first great prince of Finland ruling over his country.
4. **The Finns in the Thirty Years' War** depicts the Finnish people's struggle to survive amidst the turmoil.
5. **The Great Hostility** depicts a prior era of Russian hostility against Finland (from 1714 to 1721).
6. **Finland Awakes** depicts the future rise of Finland to overthrow Russian rule.

The final two works were frequently re-performed throughout the Finnish country, though often under pseudonyms, so as not to attract attention from the Russian censors. Eventually, Sibelius combined these two ("The Great Hostility" and "Finland Awakes") into a new tone poem entitled, simply, "Finlandia." This became his great nationalistic triumph.

The climax of Finlandia is found in the so-called hymn at the end of the work. Though perceived to be a Finnish folk tune, it is a composition original to Sibelius and has since been adopted as a hymn in many church traditions around the world. The tune is a still, solemn, and triumphant celebration of hope in Finnish future.

26

Antonín Dvorák

THE COMPOSER OF NEW FOLK MUSIC

1841-1904

BIOGRAPHY

Antonín was born in Bohemia (now the Czech Republic) to an innkeeping family. Though it was thought he would carry on the family business, Antonin moved in with his aunt and uncle to study music at the age of 12. He eventually attended conservatory and his early career was spent teaching much and writing little.

In 1875, he was awarded a study grant from the state, which enabled him to travel and study with Brahms. It was then that he also met Brahms's publisher, who promoted Dvorák's works and published his reputation-making *Slavonic Dances.*

His renown as a composer and a teacher earned him the post of the Director of the newly-established National Conservatory of Music in New York. He moved to America in 1892 and served a short tenure, returning to Bohemia in 1895. His homesick-inspired travels across America brought great musical inspiration for a number of his most popular works, including the "American" string quartet and the symphony "From the New World." In fact, many of the melodies contained in these American-inspired works are based on birdsongs (the Scarlet Tanager in the "American" quartet) or the melodic principles of spirituals (he did not simply quote them, as is often thought to be the case in *Symphony No. 9*).

Dvorák's legacy is one of Romantic nationalism crossing political borders. His philosophy that folk music belonged to the people, but could be elevated and incorporated into classical works inspired a new generation of composers, including his student H. T. Burleigh, whose works went on to define the African American spiritual and raise its status among the American public over the next half-century.

AFRICAN AMERICAN MUSICAL NATIONALISM

Throughout Dvorák's travels, he was a practicing ethnomusicologist-composer. He collected various folk songs and tunes and, rather than copying or quoting them, analyzed the works and used their melodic principles to write new works. He is quoted as saying "I tried to write only in the spirit of those national American melodies." The fact that Dvorák considered African American spirituals as "national American melodies" provides a different perspective from that of many Americans at the time, who considered the African American cultural heritage as second-class.

Dvorák emphasized the treasury that was the spirituals. Here, the distinction between country and nation is important, as the common inherited culture among many African Americans at this time derived from a history of slavery in America; therefore, the unique musical contribution made in the first decades after the Civil War often relied on the spirituals of America. Dvorák (and Burleigh after him) saw these as America's contribution to the Great Conversation in music and wrote music in the vein of these great and enduring works.

SYMPHONY NO. 9, "FOR A NEW WORLD"

Dvorák's *Symphony No. 9* was written during his tenure at the at the Conservatory in 1893. However, the work was written during his American tours while he was in Spillville, Iowa. The piece consists of four movements, all of which are based on themes that have now become cultural touchstones.

Titled "From the New World," the symphony is a microcosm of the music and culture Dvorák experienced during his time in America. The first and second movements imitate themes from spirituals, the second and third movements take after indigenous culture as portrayed in popular culture at the time, and the final movement recapitulates the themes from the first three. "I have not actually used any of the [Native American] melodies. I have simply written original themes embodying the peculiarities of the [Native American] music, and, using these themes as subjects, have developed them with all the resources of modern rhythms, counterpoint, and orchestral colour." He frequently utilizes the pentatonic scale, syncopation, and dotted rhythms to emphasize the non-classical character of the works.

The second and third movements were specifically inspired by Henry Wadsworth Longfellow's poem *Hiawatha*. In particular, ther third movement was "suggested by the scene at the feast in Hiawatha where the [Native Americans] dance." (An excerpt of the poem is included in Appendix F.)

Contrary to popular belief, Dvorák newly composed each of these themes for the symphony, even the theme to the second movement, now known widely as "Goin' Home." In fact, the lyrics were later written by a student of Dvorák, and the combination became widely popular in America, which led to the belief that is was a pre-existing spiritual.

27

Aaron Copland

THE COMPOSER OF AMERICA

1900-1990

BIOGRAPHY

Aaron Copland was born to Jewish immigrants in New York, though not in accord with the caricature delivered at the time. His mother's family came most recently from Texas and she delivered the West's most popular tunes to her son when he was just a child. Even as a teen, Copland knew he wanted to become a composer and set his studies in order to ensure his success. One of the most influential decisions he made was to settle down in Fontainebleu, France and study with one of the least-respectable sorts of teachers of the day — a woman!

Fortunately for Copland, his friend insisted he take a lesson with Nadia Boulanger, the most widely successful composition teacher of the 20th century. Boulanger shaped many of the greatest modern composers; Aaron Copland was merely her first American student, though she recognized a great genius in him.

Copland took his newfound appreciation for harmony and

innovation, learned from Boulanger, and began to synthesize an American sound. He envisioned that American classical music might become as popular as jazz or folk music. While his vision did not entirely pan out, his influence on the American public was profound. His ballet score "Appalachian Spring" is one of the most instantly-recognizable pieces of American classical music, as was his "Portrait of Lincoln" in its day (still a popularly performed, though lesser-known work). His film scores are also numerous and show his capacity for drama in music and for innovative scoring.

Toward the end of his life, Copland began experimenting with the dodecatonal system popularized by the Second Viennese School, after which point his music dropped out of the public eye and he eventually ceased composing and took up conducting full-time. He died at the age of 90, having shaped the landscape of modern music through his composition, conducting, and philosophy of music.

AMERICAN NATIONALISM

Copland's desire to make American classical music immensely popular forced him to connect with the American public in his music. At the time, there was no distinct "American sound" to music — no single idiomatic music had yet taken hold of the populus.

Copland used the influence of Mexico's highly-popular folk music style to determine how to write "American" music. After a careful analysis of American folk music, including that of the Appalachian subculture, Copland discovered the recurring use of the interval of a fifth — easily heard on a violin in the process of tuning the strings (which are tuned to open fifths) or in most American fiddle music.

By reaching into America's past, Copland discovered and set forth a vision for America's musical future, largely based on one interval — the fifth.

APPALACHIAN SPRING

Set in Pennsylvania in the 19th century, Copland's *Appalachian Spring* is among his most recognizable works and depicts a quintessentially American celebration of American life in an American setting; it's perfectly "Copland."

While Copland's early career did not tend towards popular appeal, his efforts to reach mass audiences were successful in the 1940s and '50s; so much so that he was commissioned by one of America's leading choreographers to write a suitable ballet for his orchestration. After turning down multiple classically-rooted stories, Copland agreed to set the story of *Appalachian Spring*.

The story unfolds through eight scenes: the Pioneer Woman (Mother) surveys the land, her daughter (the Bride)dances with her love (the Husbandman), the Bride and Husbandman are wed, the audience views daily life in the town, a Revivalist enters the town and preaches against the sins of the day (bringing the woes of the Civil War to the front), the Husbandman goes off to fight, the townsfolk are distressed, and finally we see the Sabbath Day on which the Husbandman returns and dances another duet with the Bride.

While most of the story revolves around celebrating American life and the celebrations in American lives (daily life, weddings, Sabbath worship, etc.), the background tension of the Civil War keeps the work from being frivolous or too light. At the same time, Copland's orchestral brilliance shines in the ordinary — the mundane activities, the Lord's Day routine, and the happiness of building a home together are all accompanied by folk-inspired music or folk music itself: nothing more, nothing less.

Most well-known of the ballet is the theme and variations on "Simple Gifts," a Shaker hymn from the 19th century. While Copland inserts the main theme from the hymn early on in the ballet, the full melody is used toward the end of the work to great effect.

While the original ballet was scored for a chamber ensemble of double string quarter, bass, flute, clarinet, bassoon, and piano; the orchestral suite was expanded later on and makes for a striking listening activity. Copland's clever use of timbre in the variations creates an excellent opportunity to discuss the role of timbre and experimentation in the early 20th century. Discussion can also focus on the simplicity of the music and the role of folk music in Copland's career. Nevertheless, one ought also to consider that sometimes beautiful music is allowed to be just that.

V

Modernism

THE AGE OF EXPERIMENTATION

CA. 1900 - PRESENT

28

Introduction

MODERNISM

The twentieth century was one of the greatest periods of worldwide upheaval in all of history. Because of the increased connection across the globe, many of the momentous decisions and events of the era impacted the citizens of many countries and regions. While this is true for the many devastatingly negative events, it is also true of the positive and neutral. Philosophies, political theories, art movements, and much more spread rapidly in this century of innovation in the wake of two Industrial Revolutions.

Modernism includes as a basic tenet the need for experimentation, largely in an effort to distinguish it from the past. James Joyce and Virginia Woolf began to navigate and establish the genre of "stream of consciousness" writing. Samuel Beckett wrote absurdist plays by the handful. E. E. Cummings did away with writing conventions in hundreds of poems. Literature was clearly seeking a new means of expression through experimentation.

The arts had also been creeping up to this new world stage with a variety of experiments. Richard Strauss's innovative and exploratory operas were deeply psychological — a reflection of their late 19th century Austrian origin. In the age of Freud and Jung, no subject area was off-limits due to Victorian puritanical social mores, nor was any subject safe from psychological evaluation or encoding. Artists began to be obsessed with the materials of composition (the medium itself and its component parts, such as canvas, paint, line, or color) as well as, or occasionally in lieu of, the subject of the work of art. (Put another way, the instruments of creativity became the subjects of creativity.) This sort of experimentation became common in the musical arts, as well.

Composers began to use the varied philosophies of the century as springboards for their thoughts on the use and usefulness of music. Music was constructed to reflect political ideologies, religious themes, or to celebrate the elements of music themselves. These extreme levels of experimentation ultimately drove many away from the classical side of music and toward its more "popular" forms, such as jazz. As composers neglected audiences, audiences returned the favor.

Almost every form of modernism would be echoed in music: Expressionism, Impressionism, Cubism, Primitivism, Futurism, Constructivism, Maximalism, Minimalism and more would all find their way into musical outlets thanks to the creative endeavors of various composers. Due to the modern proximity to these movements, audiences are still waiting to discover which of these will endure; but all of them have left some mark on the music-historical landscape.

CHARACTERISTICS OF MODERNIST MUSIC

Musical characteristics of the period reflect the philosophical characteristics of the era. As artists were dedicated to **experimentation** in every other medium, so were composers. Though such experimentations in the past often had limited ability to affect others, the connectivity of the modern world enabled the rapid spread of many of the musical innovations of the era. Because of this, **traditional music and instruments** also gained acclaim in places they might never have before. As composers experimented with the elements of music, timbre became one of the most useful technical elements to employ in experimentation, so the use of **extreme timbres** becomes a defining characteristic of this period. Finally, as philosophy travels the world and weighs heavily on the worldviews of many, it also shifts the purpose and creation of music in the minds of many composers who would write **philosophically-influenced works**.

Experimentation
World Music Influences
Timbral Extremes
Philosophical Music

MAJOR COMPOSERS

Debussy

Claude Debussy (1862-1918) was one of the leading French composers of his day. A student of the Paris Conservatoire at the age of 10, he was influenced by the spread of world music and of the literary movements of the day. He largely rejected traditional compositional boundaries and his music was characterized by the blurring of boundaries between traditional and modern. As such, his works were labeled as "Impressionistic" (a label he rejected). His most famous works are his opera *Pelléas et Mélisande* and his orchestral suites.

Stravinsky

Igor Fyodorovich Stravinsky (1882-1971) was a leading composer of the modernist era and has been referred to as "The Chameleon" of classical music. With great works in almost every genre and style of the century, Stravinsky's early Russian nationalistic ballets transformed into primitivist songs, followed by neo-classical orchestral works (and his most famous opera) and experimental serialist works. A leader in experimentation, Stravinsky's influence extended to almost every composer of the century through his powerful and influential stylistic innovation. *The Rite of Spring* is perhaps the most widely acknowledged, largely because of the famous riot it sparked at its premiere.

Schönberg

Arnold Schönberg (1874-1951) was one of the most controversial figures of the 20th century musical scene. He began his career experimenting with Romantic style under the influence of Strauss and Zemlinsky and ventured into the realm of atonality (what he called "dodecatonality") in the early part of the 1900s. His philosophical investigations opened up a new world of music theory, influencing later composers in the Second Viennese School (Berg and Webern) and beyond. His most famous work is likely the song set *Pierrot Lunaire*, though almost of his works have attained a cult-like status because of their distinct style and influence.

29

Claude Debussy

IMPRESSIONIST COMPOSER

1862-1918

BIOGRAPHY

Claude Debussy (pronounced "klode duh-byoo-see") was born to French parents in a small town near Paris. His family was forced to flee their hometown when he was just five years old to find refuge from the Franco-Prussian War. Shortly thereafter, even amidst the difficult times of war, his musical talent was discovered and he began taking piano lessons at the age of seven. At 10, he was admitted to the Paris Conservatoire, where he remained for the next 11 years.

His earliest works pushed against the traditions that he believed had confined music. He believed that many orchestral instruments were underutilized and continued the revolutionary orchestration ideas of Berlioz.

His latter years were filled with composition, writing critiques and reviews, and travelling internationally for the performances of his works. His private life was equally full — a near constant-stream of affairs filled his early days until the birth of his only daughter in 1905. He was influenced by the modern ideas of music, but not by many modern composers (he expressed a particular dislike for Wagner). He completed only opera in his lifetime, but *Pelléas et Mélisande* is considered a hallmark of the 20th century.

Debussy died at the age of 55 of rectal cancer after receiving one of the first colostomies in history.

IMPRESSIONISM

While Debussy did not like the term "Impressionist" to describe his music, the term (most frequently associated with art) is not inappropriate to describe his musical work.

His works are clear, dramatic illustrations of their subject; but they only ever evoke, rather than illustrate point-for-point. Where Wagner and others of his age sought to depict every action in the orchestra, Debussy wanted to convey the emotional intent of a piece of music or theatre without depicting each individual action. This corresponds the works of artists of this age who, rather than paint with clear lines and concrete forms, desired to convey the general shape or scope of the subject — to create an impression. The term was coined by Monet in his famous painting "Impression, Sunrise" from 1872 (pictured right).

Debussy's orchestral effects were used similar to the unique paint strokes of the Impressionist painters: always communicating, never defining. In this way, Debussy's classic works established a new form of composition which left much to the imagination and work of both performer and audience.

LA MER

Solidifying Debussy's reputation as a modernist (Impressionist) composer, La Mer (The Sea) is still recognized as one of the composers greatest works. It was coolly received at its 1905 premier (the public reception of the piece is often said to have been tainted by the public's awareness that Debussy was preparing to divorce his wife to flee with his mistress). However, a few short years galvanized his reputation and by 1908 this group of "three symphonic sketches" was a modern classic.

Debussy titled the sketches as follows:

1. De l'aube à midi sur la mer ("From dawn to midday on the sea")
2. Jeux de vagues ("Play of the waves")
3. Dialogue du vent et de la mer ("Dialogue between wind and the sea")

It is these concepts he seeks to convey in his orchestrations.

Where previous composers sought to convey the movement of water through the constant use of strings, employing the percussion, and demonstrating human involvement with the force of nature; Debussy was more highly concerned with the standalone character of the ocean through similarly organic orchestral use.

Debussy blurred lines in various aspects of the composition: melodies and rhythms are indistinct, arising from previous melodic sentiments; instruments are not used in traditional manners or for traditional purposes; even the rise and fall of each movement is more determined by the general characteristic of the scene being portrayed than by any dramatic action. One critic wrote of the premier: "The audience seemed rather disappointed: they expected the ocean, something big, something colossal, but they were served instead with some agitated water in a saucer." This was Debussy's impression of the ocean, not that of the Romantics. This paved the way for other innovations later in the century; La Mer is sometimes referred to as "the greatest symphonic work of the twentieth century."

"CLAIR DE LUNE"

"Clair de lune" remains one of the most popular piano pieces ever written. Translated as "moonlight," the piece takes its name from a poem of the same name by the famous French Symbolist poet Paul

Verlaine. Debussy also set the poem to music for voice and piano on two other occasions, but his piano work is probably the most famous.

Setting the scene of a moonlit night through the use of indistinct rhythms and a blending of pitch (thanks to the still-relatively-new *sostenuto* pedal on the piano), Debussy lines out the emotional thrust of the Verlaine poem. Interestingly, Debussy initially titled this movement "Promenade sentimental," or "sentimental dance."

It is somewhat melancholic in its use of blurred rhythms, moderate pitches without extremes, and very much gives an impression of the poem's subject: the melancholy of a soul. (The text is not provided as Symbolist poems are notoriously difficult to interpret — it is, perhaps, more helpful to hear it read and translated and move to listening.)

30

Igor Stravinsky

CHAMELEON COMPOSER

1882-1971

BIOGRAPHY

Igor Fyodorovich Stravinsky was born outside of St. Petersburg to a family of musicians. His father was a professional classical singer who had a working relationship with Russia's leading orchestral composer: Nicolai Rimsky-Korsakov.

Rimsky-Korsakov became Stravinsky's composition teacher in the earliest decade of the 20th Century, leading the young composer in his orchestral exploration and in the tradition of Russian Romanticism (in the vein of Tchaikovsky, Borodin, and others).

Following his success in Paris and the impact of his revolutionary philosophy of music, Stravinsky moved to America and continued his developmental work in every musical genre: instrumental, song, opera, ballet, symphony.

Stravinsky and Schoenberg were seen as opposing sides of the modern musical struggle, with Stravinsky diametrically opposed to

Schoenberg's system of dodecatonal serialism. Of note is the fact that Stravinsky began to experiment with serial compositional techniques after Schoenberg's death; but never let his tone rows exceed five or seven notes. Stravinsky was concerned with the furthering of musical thought, but his musical always remained rooted in some form of tradition.

THE FOUR STAGES OF STRAVINSKY

Stravinsky's music is generally divided into four main stages or periods: nationalistic, primitivistic, neo-Classical, and serial.

Nationalistic: Stravinsky's earlier music emphasized Romantic ideals: nationalistic narratives, lush orchestration, traditional rhythms and instrument use. These earlier works generally received well by the public and made a name for Stravinsky.

Primitivistic: In this era of the composer's career, modern philosophical concepts played into his compositions. Here, percussion and experimental rhythms dominate; the use of extremes of instrumental timbres often carry a pre-historic flavor, and the concept of "proper" in music is dismissed.

Neo-Classical: Stravinsky largely invented the superimposition of Classical Era structures onto modern harmonies and textures. Several of his works fall into this short period, most notably his opera The Rake's Progress, a work which deserves more attention than it generally receives.

Serial: With much experimentation toward the end of his life, Stravinsky dipped his toe into the waters of serialism. He still held some view of tonal hierarchy and structured pieces more simply, moving toward a musical climax, which Schoenberg would never have approved.

THE RITE OF SPRING

Stravinsky's life in Paris centered on his work at the *Ballets Russes*, where he premiered a number of his most famous ballets, including the piece that catapulted him to fame: *L'Oiseau de feu — The Firebird.* Based on a Slavic folk tale and inspired by Russian nationalistic music, Stravinsky's ballet galvanized his relationship with Sergei Diaghalev (the impresario of the ballet company).

Following on the success of The Firebird, Stravinsky was commissioned to write a new ballet that reflected the public's perception of the composer's home country. The popular idea regarding primitive Russia was that ancient Slavic peoples were simple barbarians, bound to pagan rituals and dark magics. While the narrative of human sacrifice appears to be untrue regarding Russian history, the fascination with ancient cultures and pagan rituals was a driving force behind Parisian high society. Diaghalev sought to exploit this in Stravinsky's next ballet: *Le Sacre du Printemps* or *The Rite of Spring*. Stravinsky and a Slavic History expert, Nicolas Roerich, wrote the scenario for a work that would change ballet forever.

The story centers on an ancient tribe preparing to welcome Spring by appeasing the god of the earth. The proper ritual includes prayers and confrontations and conclude in the annual ritual of selecting a maiden who will dance herself to death as a sacrifice to the earth: something slightly different from the run-of-the-mill Nutcracker assumed by most audiences.

Stravinsky's transformation of music is apparent from the opening bars of the piece. The iconic bassoon solo disoriented listeners at the premier for its foreign timbre. The heavy arsenal of percussion instruments and their seemingly-random percussive strikes in the opening dance also crushed the audience's sense of orientation. Where traditional ballet focused on the lightness of the dancers and upward movement, Najinsky's choreography emphasized heaviness, jerky movements, and downward motion.

The score settles into patterns of bitonality and polyrhythms, and does so years before either became popular elements of modernist music. This apparent disregard for traditional keys and meters caused a great upheaval in the theatre. Much of the upper class audience was appalled by the music and chaos. Many of the *avante-garde* crowd adored what was happening in the music and on stage. This led to the most famous riot in music: forty audience members were arrested for assault. Multiple duels had been arranged. The audience spilled out into the street in revolt.

Stravinsky never let up: the piece rolled on in utter turmoil and unfolded into the extraordinary upending of classical music. Or so it seemed: the piece was performed without the dancing in the next years and was received by popular acclaim.

Stravinsky had achieved not only notoriety, but transformation: few pieces of music in the remainder of the century would be untouched by *Le Sacre du Printemps.*

31

Arnold Schönberg

MATHEMATICAL COMPOSER

1874-1951

BIOGRAPHY

Arnold Franz Walter Schönberg was born to a Jewish family in Vienna in the middle of the Romantic era and marinated in the cultural aesthetics of the era throughout his young life.

Schönberg had very little formal training — his only composing education was what little he had been taught by his friend, composer, and future brother-in-law Alexander von Zemlinsky (a well-respected late Romantic composer). Schönberg is still hailed as history's most important auto-didact composer.

Schönberg's early works are heavily influenced by Romanticism, and he always claimed influence by tradition, saying his works had "arisen entirely from the traditions of German music.... My teachers were primarily Bach and Mozart; secondarily Beethoven, Brahms, and Wagner." His later explorations of Wagnerian chromaticism and the constant pushing of the envelope led others to say that his works no longer fit the traditional mold. He is perhaps now best known as the father of "atonalism," a term he would revile.

His works passed through Romanticism and expressionism and the heavy hand of Wagner can be felt in most of these works. Schönberg continues Wagner's use of delayed resolution in music, heightening the idea to the point that not every piece of music actually resolves. In fact, he believed that when ordered correctly, the tones of a scale lose their traditional hierarchy and the idea of a singular tonal center to a piece of music fades away. Because of this, his music has been labelled "atonal," or, more properly, "pantonal" or "pan-diatonic," as all chromatic notes are absorbed into the new diatonic structure.

His influence in the twentieth century is hard to overstate, with his two most famous students — Anton Webern and Alban Berg — carrying on his tradition. His ordering of pandiatonicism led to a complete tonal revolution in the twentieth century and has lasting effects on modern composers, as well.

DODECATONALISM (SERIALISM)

Another common label for Schönberg's music is "serialist" or "dodecatonalist" (from the Greek words for "twelve" and "note"). Schönberg selected precise orders or permutations of the twelve chromatic notes in a scale and used only these notes in this order to produce a piece of music. The durations and octaves of pitches were allowed to change, but the order was in a fixed series: hence, "serial music."

Throughout the works, the pitches were allowed to be performed on a different starting note, but in the same order, tacking the skipped notes on to the end (changing the starting "number" of pitch), at a higher pitch level (transposed), moving backward through the tone row ("retrograde") or with opposite directions of notes at the same distance from the given pitch ("inverted"), or any combination of all of these. Thus, the music has a firm structure and foundation, but can be varied throughout to give varying degrees of tension and resolution.

PIERROT LUNAIRE

Pierrot Lunaire, or "Moonstruck Pierrot" or "Pierre in the Moonlight" may be Schönberg's most famous work and it was certainly his earliest work that challenged the musical norms of his age. The song cycle takes its name from the original title of a group of poems by French poet Albert Giraud, which had been translated into German (which Schönberg set). It comprises a set of 21 poems performed by singer (soprano), flute, clarinet, violin, cello, and piano — an instrumental combination which became so popular after this piece that it is now known as the "Pierrot ensemble," and has been mimicked by countless other composers.

Schönberg was approached by a retired actress, Albertine Zehme, to commission the cycle. She selected the poems and, because she was not a singer, requested that the "singer" recite the poetry to a tune at a fixed pitch, a phenomenon Schönberg had previously invented in music as *sprechstimme* or *sprechgesang* ("speaking-voice" or "speak-singing"). Because of the lack of tonal center and the use of *sprechstimme*, *Pierrot Lunaire* had mixed reactions from the audience, much like Stravinsky's *Rite of Spring*.

Schönberg pays homage to Classical music in his use of traditional structures (most pieces are organized in sonata, passacaglia, canon, or other Classical forms), and in the overall employment of the character Pierrot. Pierrot was a traditional character in Italian stage works, or masques, from the Renaissance and Baroque eras. Pierrot and Columbine are clown-like characters who often wind up in tragicomic circumstances. Here, Pierrot's love of the world is on full display as he sings of the more secular side of life: love, sex, religion (the first seven songs), violence, crime, blasphemy (the second seven songs), and the haunting of his past (the final seven songs).

While Schönberg does not utilize serial techniques in Pierrot, he does employ his love for numerology, especially the numbers 3, 7, and 13. There are three sets of seven poems, each poem has thirteen lines, with each first line being repeated three times (as lines 7 and 13). The piece is his opus 21, with 21 poems, begun on March 12, 1912. The music repeats 7-note motifs, and the ensemble, with conductor, totals 7 people. Schönberg's music is music for the early twentieth century *intelligentsia*, not the common man. At the same time, he said of the premier, "If they were musical, not a single one would give a damn about the words. Instead, they would go away whistling the tunes."

Students will likely feel unsettled listening to the piece (and not be able to whistle the tunes). This is largely because of Schönberg's avoidance of resolving harmonies, or of thinking of harmony at all. His concept of coinciding notes was the production of dissonance, not the forward momentum of harmonic structures. This is a worthwhile discussion for those new to listening to modernist works and may help students understand the music better, especially when coupled with a discussion of selected texts.

32

Blues and Jazz

AMERICA'S OWN NATIONALISM

CA. 1900 -

THE HISTORY OF BLUES AND JAZZ

While the works of such modernist composers as Stravinsky and Schönberg tended to drive the public away from classical music, there were composers who helped the popular culture orient themselves toward serious composers. Ironically, this eventually developed into such a divide that the composers to follow are not typically thought of as "classical" by nature. The branches of the music tree began to grow so far apart that even those genres originally conceived as similar or as wildly different began to separate or collide in strange new ways.

Jazz is a strange and uniquely American phenomenon that has now become an international musical conversation. Jazz has its roots in the American South, largely brought out of a handful of musical characteristics from West African slaves in the nineteenth century. Thus, Jazz is actually a derivative of non-American folk music. As men and women were sold into slavery on plantations and in homes, many slaveowners felt it was necessary to educate these people with Christianity (an idea that eventually added to the "White Saviour" complex of many in the Civil War-era South), and felt they were really doing good to the people they bought and sold as property, because they could provide hope for the eternal future, even if they weren't doing it for the present.

Many of the slaves who were taught Christianity did not adopt it as an exclusive religion, but became syncretist (adding Christianity to folk religion or adopting other practices alongside Christian worship practices), and the Christian music of African Americans took on a life of its own. Call-and-Response elements became commonplace in religious services of many historically black churches, and the use of the pentatonic scale (the set of five pitches that forms a scale widely used in traditional music) became the building block of many new tunes.

Many songs were sung while working or worshipping that would sound theological and laudatory, and may have had that dimension, but carried a secret code for escape. Those that intentionally carried a double meaning while emphasizing the religious aspect became known as "Spirituals." Spirituals were songs with hope, while the "blues" were songs generally without hope. Blues songs had a typical form and refrain and could be repeated in a call-and-response fashion over and over, with different singers taking the lead position, or "caller." Songs like "Sometimes I Feel Like a Motherless Child" bear the traditional form and chord progression that would come to define not only the blues genre, but the beginnings of jazz.

CHARACTERISTICS OF JAZZ

The freedom of the so-called "12-Bar Blues" opened up new avenues for exploration among composers. Because of the performance practice tied to spirituals and blues — improvisation based on circumstance, call-and-response technique, a high degree of ensemble-based performance, the featuring of soloists, and the use of the pentatonic scale — Blues was able to quickly develop into a far-reaching and very technically progressive genre.

By combining these Blues characteristics with the elements of Ragtime and the chromatic-harmonic experiments of the early modernists like Wagner, Stravinsky, and Schönberg; composers like Joplin, Gershwin, Ellington, and others would slowly push otherwise-too-extreme musical measures into the spotlight and into the public taste. Because many early jazz composers still held to a tonal hierarchy and were writing for public appeal and because many classical composers were less concerned with the favor of the masses, what had begun as a folk idiom travelling through classical techniques and harmonies ended as one of the people's most favorite genres of the twentieth century: Jazz.

Jazz particularly hinges on two other important musical ideas, especially in jazz singing: improvisation and scat.

Improvisation: Most music is written down by a composer in advance of the performance, and the job of the performer is to play or interpret the music of the composer. Jazz turned over the role of composer to the perrformer, at least at key moments, so that a person's individual skills and musical expression could come to the forefront. The natural progression of the nineteenth century virtuoso, jazz players with "chops" would rule the day in the twentieth century. Later composers would give the barest of outlines to their performers and would use this as an opportunity to improvise together and experiment. (One rarified example of this was the recording of Miles Davis's album, "Kind of Blue," for which band members received one page of musical sketches and recorded the entire 45-minute album in just a few takes on two separate days.)

Scat: As vocalists joined the fray of performing jazz, they also had the opportunity to solo, but inventing words in the heat of the moment became difficult. Jazz singers utilize neutral syllables that imitate the sounds of jazz instruments (trumpet, drum, bass, saxophone, etc.) and thus give voice to their musical expressions.

33

Scott Joplin

MASTER OF THE RAG

1868-1917

BIOGRAPHY

Scott Joplin was born in Texas and grew up in the age of Brahms and high Romanticism, studying the piano to become a concertist. He quickly gained renowned as a traveling pianist and began a relationship with a music publisher in St. Louis. His original compositions were outrageously successful as the first works in his own new genre: ragtime.

Later in life, he moved to New York City, where he was able to write about his developments in his book The School of Ragtime. In it, he outlined the principles of ragtime music which had gained him such notoriety and established a wave of copycats across the United States.

Much of his later life was spent in attempting to establish himself as a "real" composer (that is, a composer more in the classical than in the popular vein), with most of his efforts poured into his three-act opera *Treemonisha*. Seldom performed now, Joplin was convinced it would become successful and had a mental breakdown over the stresses of its repeated failure. He was institutionalized a year before his death.

Joplin remains one of America's most iconic composers for pieces like "Maple Leaf Rag" and "The Entertainer" (which was featured in the hit film, "The Sting"). Most of all, Joplin ought to be remembered as the founding member of the school of jazz.

CHARACTERISTICS OF RAGTIME

Ragtime is based on three basic elements, all of which were relatively well-utilized in music prior to Joplin's developments, but had never come together in a unified presentation: complex bass patterns, sporadic syncopation, and stop-time breaks.

Complex bass patterns: Many are familiar with the arpeggiations or Alberti bass lines of Classical-era composers. These are simple lines that outline the harmonies used in the piece. Joplin's bass lines often outline the harmonies, but frequently use non-chord tones and have melodies that seem to speak on their own. They are rhythmically and harmonically complex and drive the music to new levels of energy and expression.

Sporadic syncopation: Rather than counting strictly "ONE and TWO and THREE and FOUR and" in the music, syncopation places the emphasis off the beat: "one AND two AND three AND four AND." Joplin's music used a combination of both of these without a strict regularity, which increased the energy level of the music and surprises the listener.

Stop time breaks: Joplin's music often breaks for complete silence to interrupt the rhythmic flow and arrest the audience's attention. Occasionally used in prior composers, Joplin's music makes this an exciting habit.

34

Louis Armstrong

MASTER OF THE TRUMPET

1901-1971

BIOGRAPHY

Louis Armstrong grew up in the heartland of American blues and jazz: New Orleans. His exposure to the sounds of Dixie Land built a love of music that endured from early childhood — he dropped out of school in fifth grade to work a job that gave him the money for his first cornet.

"Satchmo"'s (so called by his mother for the inflation of his cheeks when he played: they looked like a "Satchel mouth") first professional experiences came in the juvenile home in which he was detained for an infraction when he was 12; he was leader of the brass band, which led him to his next post with Joe "King" Oliver, the renowned brass soloist in New Orleans. Oliver led him to Chicago, where the two built up a reputation as band leaders and dueling soloists. It was not long before Louis broke out on his own, eventually leading The Hot Seven for decades, recording some of the most influential albums in early jazz.

Armstrong's incredible gifting for soloing and scatting made him a worldwide phenomenon — he was frequently referred to as "Ambassador," and even simply "Pops." His indomitable joy, unmistakable voice, and reverie-like blues solos have maintained his place as a fixture of American jazz throughout the century.

THE SOLOIST

Early jazz music was based on ensemble performances: New Orleans jazz was based on the classic Dixie Land ensemble, Chicago-based Joe Oliver recorded with the whole ensemble around a microphone, and big bands were the swing-based holdovers of classical orchestras. When Armstrong hit the scene, his unique style moved the stellar front man into the limelight.

Where previous bands were based on the skill of the bandleader in holding the ensemble together and writing interesting big band arrangements, Louis Armstrong turned this idea on its head, with his own interesting improvisations, his singing style, his newfound "scatting," and his electric personality and charm.

What was perhaps most effective was his interesting blend of musical styles. His lyrical playing and narrative-like solos were a unique form of expression not seen in most soloists of the day, few as they were. Many instrumentalists, trumpeters, cornetists, and trombonists alike — modeled their playing after various aspects of Armstrong's style. This growing trend solidified the fame of Armstrong, but also the role of the virtuosic soloist in America's jazz.

35

Edward "Duke" Ellington

THE MAKER OF THE ENSEMBLE

1899-1974

BIOGRAPHY

Born and raised in Washington, D. C., Ellington grew up on music. He began piano lessons at the age of 11 and was writing his own music in his teen years. The high society manners and grace taught to him by his mother and her friends combined with his dapper appearance led his childhood friend to grace him with the nickname "Duke."

Aged 14, he wrote his first piece by ear, "Soda Fountain Rag," and continued to improvise based on principles of genres he picked up by ear, saying ""I would play the 'Soda Fountain Rag' as a one-step, two-step, waltz, tango, and fox trot.... Listeners never knew it was the same piece." Before the age of 25, he was regularly performing at the prominent jazz venue The Cotton Club and had already become the leader of "Duke Ellington and His Orchestra."

A lifelong collaborator and composer, Ellington was committed to writing and performing the music of his band members through the entire duration of his life. He would frequently pay band members for snippets of melodies he thought would fit into a new tune he was writing, and had such a mind for melodic invention that many of his biggest tunes were written down in less than an hour's time.

Ellington had a brilliant mind for composing, but was not so arrogant as to think he could not benefit from working with others. His collaborative spirit means his name is on over 1000 compositions, making him one of the most prolific composers America has ever produced. He also did not write music that all fits in one style — his works span rag, swing, bebop, and a pastiche orchestral work: *Black, Brown, and Beige.*

Ellington ushered in the age of high class jazz and then disbanded the boundaries of genre, calling his music simply "American."

"TAKE THE 'A' TRAIN"

Billy "Swee' Pea" Strayhorn was Ellington's career-spanning collaborator. Together, the two would write many of Ellington's greatest hits, both men entirely in sync when it came to melodic interpretation, harmonic improvisation, groove, and lyrical genius (Strayhorn's specialty when it came time to adapt instrumental numbers for singers).

Strayhorn reportedly wrote the song after he was first hired by Ellington. Duke's instructions to his home in New York began with "Take the 'A' Train," referring to the new subway line which would take the Pennsylvanian newcomer to Ellington's home on the affluent Sugar Hill in Harlem.

The piece became the band's theme tune after a legal battle with the rights and licensing group ASCAP and became synonymous with Ellington and His Orchestra, even as it was adapted, sung, re-performed, and transformed by countless other musicians over many decades, all inspired by Ellington and Strayhorn.

BLACK, BROWN, AND BEIGE

In 1943, Ellington premiered the longest and most-anticipated work of his storied career. Over the prior three decades, Ellington had built a name as one of America's greatest composers, most brilliant pianists, and a prominent figure in the African American community. Ellington's new orchestral suite — *Black, Brown, and Beige* — would be an opportunity to hear jazz orchestral sounds telling the story of the African American experience, all from the perspective of an African American composer.

As the star-studded audience settled in, they were unsure of what to expect from the jazz band leader's symphonic suite. Many expected a more classically-minded composition and left deriding the suite for its lack of traditional grounding. Many were more progressively-minded, ready to accept the jazz notions of the work, but curious why it was rooted in the traditional orchestra. Some had no room in their definition of music for African American activism, still others were shocked that Ellington did not maximize the opportunity to speak out against current cultural trends. There was no pleasing America at the time, but *Black, Brown, and Beige* has become one of Ellington's most well-respected works after the passing of time.

The work is in three movements, each with three sections, organized as follows:

I. Black: Work Song, Come Sunday, Light
II. Brown: West Indian Dance, Emancipation Celebration, Blues Theme Mauve
III. Beige: Various Themes, Sugar Hill Penthouse, Finale

"Black" is a testament to the African heritage of African Americans. It opens with a tom-tom beat that never disappears, reminiscent of tribal drums, carried to America, where riffs of spirituals drift in and out of the melody. The second section brings to the forefront a spiritual tune written by Ellington (the vocal version, performed with Mahalia Jackson, became a standalone hit in the 1960s), with the third section foreshadowing the increasingly joyous outlook of former slaves after the Civil War.

"Brown" is a reflection of the service of African Americans in American history, particularly their contributions to the Revolutionary and Civil Wars, and their succeeding emancipation. The movement is finished off with a blues theme, showing the remaining work to be done in the Antebellum South, progressing toward the coming Civil Right Movement.

"Beige" is a somewhat ironic or sarcastic take on the veneer of equality that existed in the 1940s. In a sense, he was saying the only way a black man could be treated equally was to make him "beige" (or, more white than dark). This movement seems more in line with the upper class New York society in which the piece was heard, than it does with much of black America. Ellington's work stood tall then and stands as a reminder of the history of African Americans to this day.

VI

Musical Theatre

THE ENTERTAINMENT OF THE PEOPLE

CA. 1900 -

36

Introduction

THE HISTORY OF MUSICAL THEATRE

Musical theatre, as distinct from opera, does not necessarily have a start date. While opera was popular for centuries, its cousin grew right alongside it. Some of the earliest operas were performed alongside *masques* — performances of song and poetry. Mozart's *The Magic Flute* was actually billed as a *singspiel* — a sung play. And, of course, Johann Strauss and the famous pair of Gilbert and Sullivan were making operettas in the latter part of the nineteenth century.

Operetta is perhaps the clearest precursor to modern musical theatre. As operatic fare grew longer, darker in tone, and heavier in subject matter, some audiences wanted comic relief and operetta provided just that. Operetta retains the large orchestra, the mostly-singing format, and the "serious" classical compositional grounding. But operetta tells simple and light-hearted stories and leaves plenty of room for witty jokes and slapstick comedy in its spoken intervals.

One opera house in Paris began to include other routines into its nightly performance schedule. *Folies Bergère* became a performance hall for comic opera, operettas, songs, and performative acrobatics and gymnastics (perhaps nearing the stage performances of a circus, rather than an opera house). Eventually, the routines made famous at *Folies*

Bergère began to include music hall revues. Revues were often a pastiche of song, dance, and sketch scenes (Bing Crosby's famous film *White Christmas* is perhaps one of the most famous musical revues.) The acts degenerated into an almost constant stream of women dancing and modeling in near-nothing costumes, often appearing in tableaus, posed nude. While this made its mark in Parisian culture, it also traveled across the Atlantic in the form of Florenz Ziegfeld's "Ziegfeld Follies."

Ziegfeld's work organized follies-style performances (musical revues) in America for nearly three decades, bringing on new performers each year and raising up the next generation of stars, both of beautiful American women, and of comedy and dramatic actors. Ziegfeld's "Follies" was the venue that launched a thousand careers, notably those of W. C. Fields, Will Rogers, Eddie Cantor, Gilda Gray, and Fannie Brice.

As musical revues became the norm in some stretches of America, vaudeville theatre had made its mark with similar routines, but as a cleaner variety show, sometimes incorporating acrobats, jugglers, monologues, and song and dance. Vaudeville eventually morphed into a more story-telling form before it lost its share of audiences due to the poverty of the Great Depression and the advent of "talkies" — films with accompanying sound (as opposed to silent films). Talkies began to take up time in vaudeville shows, which now "accompanied" the movies. As radio and television became staple products, stage variety shows dwindled.

Early jazz artists writing songs in the vein of vaudeville made a splash in the music publishing industry — sheet music sales were the driving factor behind song popularity in an age prior to radio and the wide adoption of records. One block in New York City was famous for its publication of music: Tin Pan Alley. Known for its noisy out-of-tune upright pianos used to demonstrate new music (often simultaneously from various offices) sounded like tin pans being beaten in an alley. Some of the most famous composers of this genre include Scott Joplin, George M. Cohan, Harold Arlen, Irving Berlin, George and Ira Gershwin, Lorenz Hart, Richard Rodgers, Oscar Hammerstein, Cole Porter, Frank Loesser, and Hoagy Carmichael.

Musical Theatre adopted all of these forms of entertainment and rolled them into one new style, solidified by many of the later names listed above.

37

W. S. Gilbert and Arthur Sullivan

THE COMIC PAIR

1836-1911 AND 1842-1900

BIOGRAPHIES

William Schwenk Gilbert was born to a military father-turned poet and grew up writing joyous and absurd poems and plays. In his mind, the whole world could be topsy-turvy, but one must follows the rules of the world you make. And he always did. A brilliant and exacting humorist, his wit lay in social satire that some compared with fellow Englishman Jonathan Swift.

Arthur Sullivan was the son of a bandmaster and had mastered all of the instruments in his father's ensemble by age 8. His education was masterful — he was referred to as the most promising young musician in England and began an excellent career with numerous professional awards to his name.

The two worked together on 14 operettas, most of which are

still well-known and performed (especially by countless Gilbert and Sullivan Societies across the globe) and feature stock characters and absurd plots taken to their logical extremes until a *deus ex machina* saves the day.

Their working relationship lasted for years until Sullivan wanted to write more serious works and Gilbert felt he did not have the dramatic capacity for them. Their relationship dissolved, but their witty works carry on in their place.

THE PIRATES OF PENZANCE, OR THE SLAVE OF DUTY

After a numerous successes in the operatic world, Gilbert and Sullivan returned to one of their favorite themes: maritime misconduct. The Pirates of Penzance are a band of misfit orphans who refuse to attack orphans, out of duty. Their ward, Frederick, is bound to them until his 21st birthday, which is coming soon. They launch an attack on a nearby island and come to claim the victims: orphan young women in the ward of the Major-General. He knows the pirates will not hold orphans hostage and claims to be one himself; they relent, though each of them has fallen in love with one of the girls (Frederick is soon betrothed to Mabel).

In the second act, Frederick discovers he was born on February 29, technically making his 21st birthday decades away. He reveals this to the pirates and vows that upon that date, he will (out of duty) turn on the pirates in the service of the queen. He also reveals the Major-General's lie and the pirates return to capture their soon-to-be brides. All secrets come out and it is discovered that all pirates are simply "noblemen gone wrong." This known, they swear their allegiance to the crown (since they are, after all, respectable sea-faring men), and all are given their brides.

The Pirates of Penzance is an archetypical Gilbert and Sullivan show: mixed identities, concealed secrets, last-minute reversals, a simple love story, and the show-stopping "patter song" for the comic bass. It is a wonderful introduction to Gilbert and Sullivan and a great bridge from opera to musical theatre.

38

George M. Cohan

THE COMPOSER OF PATRIOTISM

1878-1942

BIOGRAPHY

George M. Cohan was born on July 3 (not July 4 as he claimed). A son of Irish immigrants who were vaudeville performers, Cohan grew up on the stage, writing his own stage works even as a teenager. As was common at the turn of the century, many Irish immigrants adopted an overly enthusiastic American spirit to compensate for the anti-Irish fervor in the eastern United States.

His shows were unique in the fact that he was not writing revues, but scripted Broadway shows, shaping the future of American musical theatre. His legacy endures today as "The Man Who Created Broadway" and as the early spirit of America.

AMERICANA SONGS

In the spirit of American song, there is none better than George

M. Cohan, whose hits include well-known songs like "Yankee Doodle Dandy," "Give My Regards to Broadway," "You're a Grand Old Flag," and "Over There."

Yankee Doodle Boy/Dandy

Perhaps George M. Cohan's most well-known song, "Yankee Doodle Boy" tells the story of a perfectly American lad and his perfectly American heritage. He loves a perfectly American girl and does perfectly American things as his pastime. Ironically, Cohan sang this song as though every aspect of it were true of himself, though his Irish heritage was a complete contradiction to the song. Still a hit today, the song perfectly fit his All-American persona.

Give My Regards to Broadway

Originally in the same musical that spawned "Yankee Doodle Boy," this song was the other hit number, also pseudo-autobiographical. In the show, one friend is sending another off to America, where the first is so certain his friend will become a hit that he sends him off the with the titular parting wish.

Over There

Written as America chose to end its policy of non-intervention, Cohan wrote "Over There" to encourage young men to enlist in the armed forces and serve during World War I. The song was an incredible hit and earned Cohan his own specially-designated medal from Congress.

39

George Gershwin

THE CLASSICAL JAZZER

1898-1937

BIOGRAPHY

Jacob Gershwine was born in New York to a Jewish family amid a season of racial tension and anti-Semitism throughout the world, including in New York. At the beginning of his musical career, he changed his name to Gershwin (as it was pronounced) and adopted his nickname, George. George learned music by ear on the piano his parents bought for his brother, Ira. In his teenage years, he left school and worked on Tin Pan Alley as a "song plugger," sight reading anything and everything put before him to sell music to publishers and recorded many piano rolls for player pianos.

George and Ira were the premier songwriting team of Tin Pan Alley, writing thousands of works in George's short lifetime. Ira was often called the "Jeweler" for his uncanny ability to write lyrical gems to the already-completed music George had given him. George wrote many musical revues, became the backbone of the Great American Songbook, and made jazz a respectable part of the classical music idiom through his experimentation and endless creativity.

RHAPSODY IN BLUE

In spring of 1924, rehearsals for George's latest musical "Sweet Little Devil" were under way and he had been asked by conductor Paul Whiteman to write a piano concerto for the orchestra he led with Gershwin at the piano. Gershwin had declined due to the short amount of time to composer, but Whiteman was already advertising the piece. With five weeks to the premier, on the train ride to rehearsal in Boston, Gershwin claims:

> "It was on the train, with its steely rhythms, its rattle-ty bang, that is so often so stimulating to a composer.... I frequently hear music in the very heart of the noise. And there I suddenly heard—and even saw on paper—the complete construction of the rhapsody, from beginning to end. No new themes came to me, but I worked on the thematic material already in my mind and tried to conceive the composition as a whole. I heard it as a sort of musical kaleidoscope of America, of our vast melting pot, of our unduplicated national pep, of our metropolitan madness. By the time I reached Boston I had a definite plot of the piece, as distinguished from its actual substance."

Gershwin never had time to write the piano part down and wound up improvising the piano part at the performance; his improvisations were later written down and have become the standard material performed.

From the opening klezmer-inspired clarinet solo to the raucous jazz blasts to the final rally, Gershwin had successfully brought jazz music into the concert hall and elevated the popular view of jazz into a refined, classical genre.

40

Irving Berlin

THE COMPOSER OF SHOW BUSINESS

1888-1989

BIOGRAPHY

Born Israel Beilin, Irving Berlin's family immigrated to American when he was just five years old. His career began early when he started busking at age 13 after his father's death. By age 23, he was an international success with his first big hit: "Alexander's Ragtime Band." Self-taught, he never learned to read or write music and his piano was famously fitted with a transposer, which allowed him to play anything in C Major and simply change the key to the singer he was accompanying.

Nearly two dozen Broadway musicals have his name on them, as well as a dozen or more film scores. He also helped found ASCAP (the music rights association) and a popular charity that receives all income from his patriotic songs, the most famous of which is "God Bless America," he received a Congressional Gold Medal for these works.

Over a thousand patriotic and Great American Songbook songs can be traced back to Berlin, songs like "White Christmas," "Puttin' On the Ritz," "Cheek to Cheek," "There's No Business Like Show Business," and "Blue Skies." Jerome Kern later said of him, "Irving Berlin has no place in American music — he *is* American music."

BLUE SKIES

One of Berlin's earlier hits, "Blue Skies" opens with a brooding, minor passage that opens up into a sometimes-sunny chorus. The piece was an instant hit when it was first used in Rodgers and Hart's musical *Betsy* — a limited-run show that, on opening night, spawned 24 encores of "Blue Skies." The following year, it was one of the first songs ever featured in a "talkie" film in Al Jolson's performance in the 1927 *The Jazz Singer*. Its wide reception continues today, as one of the most frequently performed jazz standards in the Great American Songbook, even used repeatedly in the *Star Trek* franchise. Like the mood of the piece, the song begins in minor and opens up to a major ending, reflecting the power of music and nature to change the heart, no matter the weather above or inside.

GOD BLESS AMERICA

While a stiff competition, "God Bless America" may be Berlin's best-known work. Like George M. Cohan, Berlin was a deeply patriotic immigrant to America, though his off-stage career meant that his works did not have the same veneer of gaudy patriotism, but rather a more heartfelt and reflective sort. Berlin first wrote the piece during his service in the American Army in World War I, but did not use it publicly until 1938, when his Jewish heritage became especially sensitive amid Hitler's rise to power. He reworked some lyrics and it was sung publicly on Armistice Day on live radio broadcast. This song later earned him a Congressional Gold Medal, along with his other patriotic works, for inspiring America in a time of need.

41

Cole Porter

THE COMPOSER OF BROADWAY

1891-1964

BIOGRAPHY

The grandson of a wealthy Indiana businessman, Cole Porter was prodigious; he began his musical studies at age six, wrote an operetta at 10, published his first piece at 11, and wrote hundreds of songs in his time at Yale, some of which are still sung there today. His time at Harvard Law was coupled with his time at the school's music program and he promptly moved to New York City to begin a string of hit Broadway compositions.

It was the better part of a decade before his first hit, "Let's Do It (Let's Fall in Love)" hit the charts, but the remainder of his career was extraordinarily successful. His catalog, numbering in the hundreds, was prolific; his songs are known for their wit, sophistication, grandiosity, and sparkling sense of humor. As natural as they seem to the listener, they are often decidedly difficult for the performer; it is the inseparable quality of music and words that has caused them to endure.

Porter had a horse-riding accident in 1937, which crushed both of his legs and left him invalided. Over the following twenty years, he would have 30 operations and lose one leg to amputation. He threw himself into his work as often as he could, continuing to write dazzlingly sophisticated and humorous Broadway shows and musical films, frequently collaborating with the likes of Ethel Merman and Frank Sinatra.

Perhaps his most well-known works are his perennial favorite stage works, Kiss Me, Kate and Anything Goes. Both of these show his skill in lyricism and in varied song-writing styles, as well as a high-class take on American popular song — the epitome of Cole Porter.

KISS ME, KATE

Written while bed-ridden, *Kiss Me, Kate* may be Porter's most enduring single work. Notably the first Porter musical in which most songs tie in to the plot line, it earned the first ever Tony for Best Musical. The musical's plot centers on a stage production of Shakespeare's The Taming of the Shrew in musical form. Incorporating the show-within-a-show device, a love triangle, and gangsters threatening the leading man; *Kiss Me, Kate* makes a strong showing in the Porter anthology.

The show has a number of standout pieces, with almost every number tying into the plot line. Enduring favorites include: "Another Op'nin', Another Show," "Wunderbar," "I Hate Men," "Were Thine That Special Face," "Tom, Dick, or Harry," "Brush Up Your Shakespeare," "Where Is the Life That I Led," and more.

42

Jerome Kern

THE COMPOSER OF AMERICAN MUSICALS

1885-1945

BIOGRAPHY

Born in raised in middle-class New York City, Kern studied music with his mother at an early age, then continued at the New York College of Music and studied further in Germany. His earliest work was playing piano for various publishers and adding new numbers to revived operettas — clearly a classical training mixed with Tin Pan Alley experience.

He went on to collaborate with Broadway lyricists (frequently P. G. Wodehouse of *My Man Jeeves* fame or Oscar Hammerstein II) on some of his earliest stage works, then continued his career in Hollywood. Combined, he wrote nearly 700 songs for dozens of theatrical and film presentations.

His music is most well-known for its lyrical finesse and down-to-earth harmonic structures: the music is elegant, but often seems derived from folk music, giving it an "Americana-esque" mood. His music helped Broadway transition from comic musical revues to more serious musicals, making him a sort of "serious" Gilbert and Sullivan for American audiences.

SHOWBOAT

In 1927, Ziegfeld took a chance on a new musical by Jerome Kern and Oscar Hammerstein II (of Rodgers and Hammerstein fame) collaborated to turn Edna Faber's novel, *Show Boat*, into a stage work. It would become the first American musical with a serious tone and the first major musical derived from literature.

Show Boat tells the story of the cast and crew of *Cotton Blossom*, a Mississippi River boat with live performances on board, from 1887 to 1927. These 40 years show the progression of racial tension in America and the power and grip of love on people of every stripe. The original production was quite the spectacle, with Ziegfeld pouring every financial resource into the work, which proved successful.

Perhaps best-known today for its serious depiction of racial tensions, the plot becomes rather tense when it focuses on the interracial marriage of two of the stars aboard Cotton Blossom — a radical departure from shows the preceded it on Broadway. Most American musical theatre prior to this was light-hearted and disjointed. Only a small handful of songs from *Show Boat* do nothing to forward the plot and every song is connected to the plot in some way — this is quite different from the Follies-style revues before it. The musical has been revived numerous times and the solo songs from the show are frequent show pieces for modern day opera and musical theatre singers.

Some of the most famous songs include "Make Believe," "Can't Help Lovin' Dat Man," "Bill," and "Why Do I Love You?"; but nothing meets the success of the classic low-bass song, made famous in the film adaptation by Paul Robeson: "Ol' Man River."

43

Richard Rodgers and Oscar Hammerstein II

THE COMPOSERS OF STORIES

1902-1979, 1895-1960

BIOGRAPHIES

Richard Rodgers came from a Jewish immigrant family and pursued music faithfully from a young age. His collected works number 43 Broadway musicals and over 900 songs; many of these are characteristic of their genre at the time. He and Lorenz Hart had a relatively successful Broadway career after nearly a decade of trying to break in, but laid the stage for later great works. He was the first person ever to win an Emmy, Grammy, Oscar, and Tony; and was also awarded a Pulitzer with Hammerstein for *Oklahoma!*

Oscar Hammerstein II was also a son of Jewish immigrants, though with a history in theatre: his grandfather (Oscar Hammerstein I) was a well-known impresario in Germany. After dropping out of law school, he collaborated with dozens of composers over a 40 year career, making him one of the most well-connected lyricists of the century.

Prior to Oklahoma!, the two tended to work with their own partners. Rodgers had created many musical scores to the lyrics of Lorenz Hart, who had slipped into alcoholism became incapable of the work load. Hammerstein previously had a successful career working with Jerome Kern on numerous stage works, but Kern didn't feel the subject matter was suitable. When Rodgers and Hammerstein were paired, they both were able to write in their preferred order: Hammerstein wanted to write lyrics first, but was always handed music by Kern; Rodgers wanted to set words to music, but had always been asked to write first by Hart! Finally, their partnership enabled both artists to thrive and give us the sound of American musical theatre.

OKLAHOMA!

Oklahoma! made history in American musical theatre, now know as the first "integrated" musical, meaning that every song in the show does something to advance the plot. From the first moment to the last, something new is uncovered in every piece that helps to drive the action of the story forward; this stands in contrast to the "park-and-bark" behaviour often seen in opera, and the utter disjunction of earlier musical revues. The show earned a special Pulitzer Prize after it premiered in 1943.

Oklahoma! is based on an earlier play, *Green Grow the Lilacs*, and tells the story of the courtship of Laurey and the cowboy Curly, though their relationship is in jeopardy due to the startlingly dark role of Jud Fry. With the right balance of light-hearted and serious moments, a depth of characterization previously unknown, and a fully-realized integration of plot, libretto, music, acting, and choreography, *Oklahoma!* stands as the musical theatre version of a Wagnerian opera: a work of total art, presenting an emotionally-powerful story through music (even complete with *leitmotifs*).

Oklahoma!'s success sparked a series of highly successful collaborations between Rodgers and Hammerstein, so much so that their names together are nearly synonymous with the idea of American musical theatre.

Appendices

Appendix A

These characteristics serve as a brief summary and anchor for listeners to the music of various eras.
They should be viewed as general guidelines for listening and not rules for the composers.

The Ancient Era (ca. - 1450)

Sacred Music (ca. 450-1450)
Monophony
No Instruments
Sung in Latin

Secular Music (ca. - 1450)
Monophony
Folk Instruments
Sung in Vernacular

The Renaissance Era (ca. 1450-1600)

Pleasant Harmonies
Counterpoint
Sweeping Lines
Dance Inspired

The Baroque Era (ca. 1600-1750)

Text Painting
Rhythmic Drive
Ornamentation for Emphasis
Rhetorical Form

The Classical Era (ca. 1750-1820)

Interest in Symmetry
Exploration of the Orchestra
Memorable Melodies
Elegance and Grace

The Romantic Era (ca. 1820-1900)

Story-Driven
Use of Extremes
Virtuosic
Memorable Melodies

The Modern Era (ca. 1900 -)

Timbral Extremes
World Music Influences
Experimentation
Music as Philosophy

Appendix B

The listening wheel allows a greater degree of facility when listening. The student can identify the era based on heard characteristics or listen for characteristics based on a known era.

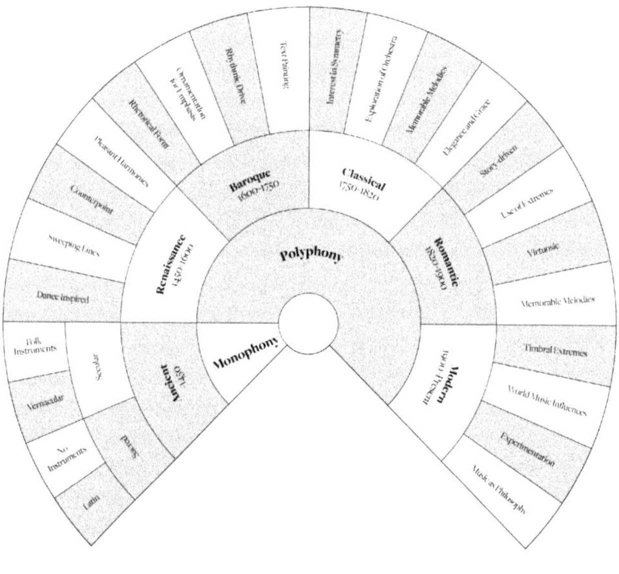

Appendix C

SCHUBERT SONG TRANSLATIONS

Gretchen am Spinnrade / Gretchen at the Spinning Wheel

This text comes from Johann Wolfgang von Goethe's telling of the story of Dr. Faustus. Margaret (or Gretchen) sits at the spinning wheel, pondering the love she enjoyed with Faust before he gave everything for great power.

Meine Ruh' ist hin, Mein Herz ist schwer
by Johann Wolfgang von Goethe
translated by John M. Punt

My peace is gone,
My heart is heavy;
I find it never
And nevermore.

Where I have him not
Is the grave to me,
The whole world
Is spoiled to me.

My poor head
Is gone mad to me,
My poor sense
Is detached to me.

My peace is gone...

I look after only him
From out the window,

I go after only him
From out the house.

His higher walk,
His noble carriage,
His smiling mouth,
His forceful eyes,

And his words's
Magic flow,
His handholding
And, ah, his kiss!

My peace is gone...

My breast longs
Only after him.
Ah, for me to grasp
And to hold him!

And kiss him
In the way I desired,
In his kisses,
I should pass away!

Erlkönig / The Shadow King

Goethe's famous poem is a brilliant work of Romanticism,illustrating the inner thoughts and emotions of the characters and their relation to the natural and supernatural world about them.

Schubert employs this to great effect in his setting of the poem for baritone and piano.

Wer reitet so spät durch Nacht und Wind?
by Johann Wolfgang von Goethe
translated by John M. Punt

Who rides so late through night and wind?
It is the Father with his child;
He has the boy wrapped in his arm,
He takes hold of him safe, he holds him warm.

"My son, why do you hide your face in fear?"
"Do you not see, Father, the Shadow-King?
The Shadow-King with crown and robes?"
"My son, it is a wisp of mist."

"You beloved child, come, go with me!
What lovely games I will play with you;
Many beautiful flowers are on the shore;
My mother has many golden garments."

"My father, my father, and do you not hear
What the Shadow-King softly promises to me?"
"Be quiet, stay quiet, my son;
The wind rustles through dry leaves."

"Will you, fine boy, go with me?
My daughters will take good care of you;
My daughters lead the nightly dance
And rock and dance and sing to you."

"My father, my father, and do you not see
The Shadow-King's daughters in the shadows?"
"My son, my son, I see it well;
The old willow tree shines so grey."

"I love you, I am excited by your lovely appearance;

And if you are not willing, by force I'll take you."
"My father, my father, he takes hold of me!
The Shadow-King has hurt me!"

The father shudders, he rides quickly,
He holds in his arms the groaning child,
He reaches the courtyard with strain and urgency;
In his arms, the child was dead.

Appendix D

SYMPHONIE FANTASTIQUE PROGRAM NOTES

These notes were written by the composer in 1845, telling the narrative of Symphonie Fantastique.

translated by John M. Punt

I. Daydreams — Passions

The author supposes that a young musician, affected by the moral malady that a celebrated writer calls the vagueness of passions, sees for the first time a woman who unites all of the charms of the ideal being of which his imagination dreams, and in this becomes madly in love. Through a singular oddity, the image of the Beloved does not present itself in the spirit of the artist except when linked to a musical thought, in which he finds a certain passionate character, but noble and timid like that which he gives to the object of his love.

This melodic reflection with its model pursues him without ceasing like a double idée fixe. This is the reason for the constant appearance, in all of the movements of the symphony, of the melody which begins the first allegro. The passage, from this state of melancholic dreaming, interrupted by some instances of joy without a subject, to that of a delirious passion, with its movements of fury, of jealousy, its returns of tenderness, its tears, its religious consolations, is the subject of the first movement.

II. A Ball

The artist is placed in the most diverse circumstances of life, in the middle of the tumult of a party, in the peaceful contemplation of the beauty of nature; but everywhere, in the city, in the fields, the beloved image comes to present itself to him and to cast trouble into his soul.

III. Scene in the Countryside

Finding himself one evening in the country, he hears in the distance two shepherds dialoguing a *ranz des vaches*; this pastoral duet, the location of the scene, the light rustling of the trees gently swaying in the breeze, some causes of hope which he has recently conceived, all combine to return to his heart an unaccustomed calm, to give his ideas a brighter color. He reflects on his isolation; he hopes soon to be no more alone. But if she cheated on him! This mixtures of hope and of fear, these ideas of happiness, troubled by some dark notions, form the subject of the adagio. At the end, one of the shepherds resumes the ranz des vaches; the other responds no more... Distant sound of thunder... solitude... silence...

IV. March to the Scaffold

Having acquired the certainty that his love is unrequited, the artist poisons himself with opium. The dose of the narcotic, too feeble to kill him, plunges him into sleep accompanied by strange visions. He dreams that he has killed the one he loves, that he is condemned, led to torture, and that he is present at his own execution. The procession advances to the sounds of a march sometimes somber and fierce, sometimes brilliant and solemn, in which a dull sound of grave footsteps succeeds without transition into the loudest bursts. At the end of the march, the first four measures of the idée fixe reappear like the last thought of love interrupted by the fatal blow.

V. Dream of a Witches' Sabbath

He sees himself at the sabbath, in the midst of an awful troupe of shadows, of sorcerers, of monsters of all species gathered for his funeral. Strange noises, moans, bursts of laughter, distant cries to which other cries seem to respond. The beloved melody reappears again, but it has lost its character of nobility and timidity; it is no more than an air of an ignoble dance, trivial and grotesque; it is she who comes to the sabbath... Roar of joy at her arrival... She joins herself in the diabolical orgy... Funeral knell, burlesque parody of the *Dies irae**, round of the sabbath. The round of the sabbath and the *Dies irae* together.

*Hymn sung in the funeral ceremonies of the Catholic Church. [HB]

Appendix E

THE LARK ASCENDING

by George Meredith

He rises and begins to round,
He drops the silver chain of sound
Of many links without a break,
In chirrup, whistle, slur and shake,
All intervolv'd and spreading wide,
Like water-dimples down a tide
Where ripple ripple overcurls
And eddy into eddy whirls;
A press of hurried notes that run
So fleet they scarce are more than one,
Yet changingly the trills repeat
And linger ringing while they fleet,
Sweet to the quick o' the ear, and dear
To her beyond the handmaid ear,
Who sits beside our inner springs,
Too often dry for this he brings,
Which seems the very jet of earth
At sight of sun, her music's mirth,
As up he wings the spiral stair,
A song of light, and pierces air
With fountain ardor, fountain play,
To reach the shining tops of day,
And drink in everything discern'd
An ecstasy to music turn'd,
Impell'd by what his happy bill
Disperses; drinking, showering still,
Unthinking save that he may give
His voice the outlet, there to live

Renew'd in endless notes of glee,
So thirsty of his voice is he,
For all to hear and all to know
That he is joy, awake, aglow,
The tumult of the heart to hear
Through pureness filter'd crystal-clear,
And know the pleasure sprinkled bright
By simple singing of delight,
Shrill, irreflective, unrestrain'd,
Rapt, ringing, on the jet sustain'd
Without a break, without a fall,
Sweet-silvery, sheer lyrical,
Perennial, quavering up the chord
Like myriad dews of sunny sward
That trembling into fulness shine,
And sparkle dropping argentine;
Such wooing as the ear receives
From zephyr caught in choric leaves
Of aspens when their chattering net
Is flush'd to white with shivers wet;
And such the water-spirit's chime
On mountain heights in morning's prime,
Too freshly sweet to seem excess,
Too animate to need a stress;
But wider over many heads
The starry voice ascending spreads,
Awakening, as it waxes thin,
The best in us to him akin;
And every face to watch him rais'd,
Puts on the light of children prais'd,
So rich our human pleasure ripes
When sweetness on sincereness pipes,
Though nought be promis'd from the seas,
But only a soft-ruffling breeze
Sweep glittering on a still content,
Serenity in ravishment.

For singing till his heaven fills,
'T is love of earth that he instils,
And ever winging up and up,
Our valley is his golden cup,
And he the wine which overflows

To lift us with him as he goes:
The woods and brooks, the sheep and kine
He is, the hills, the human line,
The meadows green, the fallows brown,
The dreams of labor in the town;
He sings the sap, the quicken'd veins;
The wedding song of sun and rains
He is, the dance of children, thanks
Of sowers, shout of primrose-banks,
And eye of violets while they breathe;
All these the circling song will wreathe,
And you shall hear the herb and tree,
The better heart of men shall see,
Shall feel celestially, as long
As you crave nothing save the song.
Was never voice of ours could say
Our inmost in the sweetest way,
Like yonder voice aloft, and link
All hearers in the song they drink:
Our wisdom speaks from failing blood,
Our passion is too full in flood,
We want the key of his wild note
Of truthful in a tuneful throat,
The song seraphically free
Of taint of personality,
So pure that it salutes the suns
The voice of one for millions,
In whom the millions rejoice
For giving their one spirit voice.

Yet men have we, whom we revere,
Now names, and men still housing here,
Whose lives, by many a battle-dint
Defaced, and grinding wheels on flint,
Yield substance, though they sing not, sweet
For song our highest heaven to greet:
Whom heavenly singing gives us new,
Enspheres them brilliant in our blue,
From firmest base to farthest leap,
Because their love of Earth is deep,
And they are warriors in accord
With life to serve and pass reward,

So touching purest and so heard
In the brain's reflex of yon bird;
Wherefore their soul in me, or mine,
Through self-forgetfulness divine,
In them, that song aloft maintains,
To fill the sky and thrill the plains
With showerings drawn from human stores,
As he to silence nearer soars,
Extends the world at wings and dome,
More spacious making more our home,
Till lost on his aërial rings
In light, and then the fancy sings.

Appendix F

FROM "XI. HIAWATHA'S WEDDING-FEAST" FROM *THE SONG OF HIAWATHA*

by Henry Wadsworth Longfellow

Then she said, "O Pau-Puk-Keewis,
Dance for us your merry dances,
Dance the Beggar's Dance to please us,
That the feast may be more joyous,
That the time may pass more gayly,
And our guests be more contented!"
Then the handsome Pau-Puk-Keewis,
He the idle Yenadizze,
He the merry mischief-maker,
Whom the people called the Storm-Fool,
Rose among the guests assembled.
Skilled was he in sports and pastimes,
In the merry dance of snow-shoes,
In the play of quoits and ball-play;
Skilled was he in games of hazard,
In all games of skill and hazard,
Pugasaing, the Bowl and Counters,
Kuntassoo, the Game of Plum-stones.
Though the warriors called him Faint-Heart,
Called him coward, Shaugodaya,
Idler, gambler, Yenadizze,
Little heeded he their jesting,
Little cared he for their insults,
For the women and the maidens
Loved the handsome Pau-Puk-Keewis.
He was dressed in shirt of doeskin,
White and soft, and fringed with ermine,

All inwrought with beads of wampum;
He was dressed in deer-skin leggings,
Fringed with hedgehog quills and ermine,
And in moccasins of buck-skin,
Thick with quills and beads embroidered.
On his head were plumes of swan's down,
On his heels were tails of foxes,
In one hand a fan of feathers,
And a pipe was in the other.
Barred with streaks of red and yellow,
Streaks of blue and bright vermilion,
Shone the face of Pau-Puk-Keewis.
From his forehead fell his tresses,
Smooth, and parted like a woman's,
Shining bright with oil, and plaited,
Hung with braids of scented grasses,
As among the guests assembled,
To the sound of flutes and singing,
To the sound of drums and voices,
Rose the handsome Pau-Puk-Keewis,
And began his mystic dances.
First he danced a solemn measure,
Very slow in step and gesture,
In and out among the pine-trees,
Through the shadows and the sunshine,
Treading softly like a panther.
Then more swiftly and still swifter,
Whirling, spinning round in circles,
Leaping o'er the guests assembled,
Eddying round and round the wigwam,
Till the leaves went whirling with him,
Till the dust and wind together
Swept in eddies round about him.
Then along the sandy margin
Of the lake, the Big-Sea-Water,
On he sped with frenzied gestures,
Stamped upon the sand, and tossed it
Wildly in the air around him;
Till the wind became a whirlwind,
Till the sand was blown and sifted
Like great snowdrifts o'er the landscape,
Heaping all the shores with Sand Dunes,

Sand Hills of the Nagow Wudjoo!
Thus the merry Pau-Puk-Keewis
Danced his Beggar's Dance to please them,
And, returning, sat down laughing
There among the guests assembled,
Sat and fanned himself serenely
With his fan of turkey-feathers.
Then they said to Chibiabos,
To the friend of Hiawatha,
To the sweetest of all singers,
To the best of all musicians,
"Sing to us, O Chibiabos!
Songs of love and songs of longing,
That the feast may be more joyous,
That the time may pass more gayly,
And our guests be more contented!

www.ingramcontent.com/pod-product-compliance
Ingram Content Group UK Ltd.
Pitfield, Milton Keynes, MK11 3LW, UK
UKHW060126010826
14089UKWH00020B/262/J

9 798869 192431